# Managing Performance
# to Maximize Results

# The Results-Driven Manager Series

The Results-Driven Manager series collects timely articles from *Harvard Management Update, Harvard Management Communication Letter,* and the *Balanced Scorecard Report* to help senior to middle managers sharpen their skills, increase their effectiveness, and gain a competitive edge. Presented in a concise, accessible format to save managers valuable time, these books offer authoritative insights and techniques for improving job performance and achieving immediate results.

## Other books in the series:

*Teams That Click*

*Presentations That Persuade and Motivate*

*Face-to-Face Communications for Clarity and Impact*

*Winning Negotiations That Preserve Relationships*

*Managing Yourself for the Career You Want*

*Getting People on Board*

*Taking Control of Your Time*

*Dealing with Difficult People*

*Managing Change to Reduce Resistance*

*Becoming an Effective Leader*

*Motivating People for Improved Performance*

*Hiring Smart for Competitive Advantage*

*Retaining Your Best People*

A Timesaving Guide

THE RESULTS-DRIVEN MANAGER

# Managing Performance to Maximize Results

• • •

Harvard Business School Press

*Boston, Massachusetts*

Copyright 2007 Harvard Business School Publishing Corporation
All rights reserved
Printed in the United States of America
11 10 09 08 07   5 4 3 2 1

Library of Congress Cataloging-in-Publication Data

Managing performance to maximize results.
    p. cm. — (The results-driven manager series)
  ISBN-13: 978-1-4221-1467-4 (pbk. : alk. paper)
  ISBN-10: 1-4221-1467-8
1. Employees—Rating of.    2. Performance—Evaluation.
3. Performance standards.    4. Employees—Coaching of.
I. Harvard Business School Press.
  HF5549.5.R3M253 2007
  658.3'125—dc22                         2007000884

# Contents

# Contents

## Leveraging 360-Degree Feedback

# Introduction

• • •

As a manager, you tackle a wide range of responsibilities. Evaluating your employees' performance arguably counts among the *most* crucial of your managerial tasks. After all, performance assessment enables you to generate valuable results for your company, including:

- Determining how well your team is meeting organizational goals

- Identifying important strengths on which your direct reports can build

- Discovering opportunities for improvement in individual subordinates' skills

- Crafting professional development plans for each of your employees

- Making key decisions about compensation, promotion, and rewards
- Documenting patterns of poor performance that protect your company from legal liability if an employee must be demoted or let go

Indeed, according to Dick Grote, author of *The Performance Appraisal Question and Answer Book: A Survival Guide for Managers*, effective performance assessment can constitute the most valuable instrument in a manager's toolbox. "No other management process," Grote maintains, "has as much influence over individuals' careers and work lives." As Grote acknowledges, a careful appraisal process can help improve an employee's performance for an entire year. And when an effective process is applied broadly across an organization, the resulting overall performance improvement can give that company a vital competitive edge. Perhaps it's not surprising that, given the strategic value of effective appraisal systems, some of the most successful firms refuse to divulge their evaluation techniques.

Yet despite these advantages, the performance assessment process, by its very nature, also contains limitations that can make evaluating employees' contributions particularly challenging. For example, delivering critical feedback during a formal performance review can demotivate the employee in question, instead of inspiring him or her to excel. "In the span of a 30-minute meeting, [a manager] can transform a vibrant, highly committed

Managers postpone formal reviews, eventually conducting a series of "wooden exercises in which what is not
said looms largest, no one suffers much discomfort, and
nothing worthwhile is accomplished," notes business
writer Monci J. Williams.

Finally, though some companies have tried to address
the limitations of traditional performance reviews by
devising innovative techniques, the resulting solutions
raise their own difficulties. Take 360-degree feedback—
whereby an individual receives input on his or her job
performance from supervisors, peers, direct reports, and
sometimes even customers or suppliers. Sounds promising, doesn't it? This rich array of feedback must be far
more comprehensive and useful than input coming
from just the employee's manager—right? Possibly. Yet
360s contain their own inherent difficulties. As just one
example, individuals who are evaluating a superior may
hesitate to provide honest impressions, for fear of retribution if their identity were to be revealed. Or an
employee who is competing with a peer over a plum
assignment or promotion may, if calculating enough,
deliberately provide a negative assessment of that peer's
performance in order to sway their manager's choice.

If all this makes you feel even more discouraged than
usual about how you can best assess your people's performance, take heart: There *are* ways to surmount the
unique challenges presented by the appraisal process.
The articles in this collection offer a wealth of ideas and
techniques for boosting the odds that your performance

employee into a demoralized, indifferent wallflower
reads the want-ads on the weekend," write Tom C
and Mary Jenkins in their book *Abolishing Perform*
*Appraisals: Why They Backfire and What to Do Instead.*

In addition, many managers find it difficult to d
mine whether they're evaluating employees' performa
accurately. Sure, anyone can recognize a true super
or a world-class slacker. But how can you be cer
you're accurately judging the contributions of 10, 2(
more direct reports—most of whom fall into the br
range between star and slacker and who are proba
performing as well as their training, tools, and w
environment allow? On a practical level alone, who
the time to conduct such a grueling analysis? And w
metrics should you use to distinguish among the ma
individuals in this group? Lacking concrete measur
any attempt to hand out individual ratings will inevital
be colored by your selective memory, emotion, and p
sonality. Moreover, you may suspect that it's importa
to customize your performance reviews for top tale
average contributors, and poor performers. But ho
precisely, should you tailor your feedback for each
these employee categories?

Thanks to these and other inherent challenges raise
by appraisal systems, managers and employees alik
often approach performance reviews with (at best) son
level of nervousness and (at worse) downright loathin
Equally troubling, negative feelings about the assessmer
process can lead to a waste of a company's valuable tim

evaluations will deliver their promised business value. Though assessing your employees' contributions will never be easy, a few changes in how you approach the process can help you turn an odious task into a productive one. In this volume, you'll find sections on overhauling your performance appraisal system for greater effectiveness; customizing performance feedback for excellent, average, and poor performers; and using the power of expectations during reviews to inspire employees to give their best on the job. Additional sections present ideas for selecting the right performance metrics for your team and for individual employees, as well as for making the most of 360-degree feedback.

Here's a quick preview of what you'll find in this book:

## Maximizing Your Performance Management System

The most effective performance appraisal systems exhibit certain shared characteristics—described in the articles that make up this section. In "Performance Appraisal Is Dead. Long Live Performance Management!" Monci J. Williams recommends replacing once-a-year, formal, manager-to-employee reviews with a two-way, continuous process of feedback, development, coaching, and goal-setting that occurs throughout the year. Through frequent exchanges, you and each of your employees identify both skill deficits and skills that your company may require of workers in the years ahead. Informed by this knowledge, employees put together plans for their own development and training that will enable them to master the desired behaviors.

The success of this approach, Williams contends, hinges on how you talk with your employees. Williams offers nine suggestions for effective communication—including conducting at least three or four performance-related conversations yearly with each employee, conveying clear expectations about the new skills and behaviors you want your direct reports to demonstrate, and delivering generous positive feedback.

"Alternatives to Performance Reviews" affirms the flaws inherent in traditional assessment systems. To surmount these flaws, the article makes a compelling case for "unbundling" the multiple functions of the traditional annual review (feedback, compensation decisions, and legal cover) and creating separate mechanisms for each function.

For example, one software firm that has abolished performance reviews expects managers and employees to conduct some kind of discussion about performance at least monthly—though employees aren't rated at those times. The sessions focus on where improvements can be made in performance and how employees can implement those improvements. Other companies handle pay decisions through a separate mechanism as well. For instance, General Motors' powertrain division awards pay increases based on an employee's experience within a given pay grade. Other companies award raises to subordinates who acquire specific new skills, or offer merit-based raises in discussions separate from feedback sessions.

In "Performance Appraisals with More Gain, Less Pain," management consultant Peter L. Allen distills key points from Dick Grote's book *The Performance Appraisal Question and Answer Book* about how to make your appraisal system more effective. Grote recommends at least two formal meetings with each employee every year—one at the beginning (to plan) and one at the end (to review). In between, Grote advises, managers "should be coaching their employees every day." Keeping a regular written log of employees' contributions can also help you better prepare for formal reviews—and prevent you from falling victim to all-too-common biases (such as focusing only on the negative or remembering only recent events). Tying performance feedback to your company's strategy and mission also helps, as does clarifying the handful of key responsibilities each employee has and evaluating his or her performance against those responsibilities.

The section concludes with "Successful Performance Measurement: A Checklist" by business writer Karen Carney. This article provides five key criteria against which to judge the effectiveness of your approach to performance assessment: (1) "Our system starts with big-picture goals—and everyone knows what they are"; (2) "Every group has performance drivers linked to the big-picture objectives"; (3) "Individual and work-group performance objectives are clear and reasonable"; (4) "We educate and coach employees continually"; and (5) "We have a clear and simple system that tracks progress toward our goals." In addition to these criteria, Carney offers three tips for assessing work that doesn't lend itself to easy quantification—such as relationship-building and creativity. Advice includes involving your employees in determining their own measurement criteria (for example, "If you weren't on this team, what wouldn't get done?"), finding qualified judges (other employees, customers, suppliers, business partners) to assess people's performance according to these criteria, and combining hard and soft metrics as appropriate.

## Handling Excellent, Average, and Poor Performers

Your star employees, average contributors, and underperformers all present different challenges at review time. The articles in this section offer recommendations for customizing your appraisals for each group. In "How to Get the Best Out of Performance Reviews," business writer Michael E. Hattersley advises conducting three kinds of reviews. With star players, "commend [them] in detail, so you can reinforce positive performance... Talk to [them] about the problems you're facing and invite [them] to participate in the solutions." With average contributors, decide whether they're working up to capacity. If so, review them kindly without raising their expectations. If not, let them know how they can improve and what the rewards will be for doing so. With poor performers, say so outright "but hold out some hope for improvement. Be as specific as you can about what's wrong and how it can be fixed." And "stick to clear performance criteria rather than attack the subordinate's personality, which isn't likely to change."

In "Performance Management That Drives Results," business writer Loren Gary provides additional guidelines from human resource experts for evaluating and managing your three groups of employees in distinctive ways. For example, identify your group's "A jobs"—those positions that link most directly to your company's strategy. For each A job, determine what defines top performance. Put your best people in those roles, and evaluate their contributions based on your definitions of excellence. Your "B players"—those whose performance meets basic expectations—also have a role in your team. But until they demonstrate that they can perform at A levels, don't put them in A jobs. As for "C players" (underperformers), "more and more businesses are culling their bottom ranks of employees with good results," notes Mark Huselid, professor of human resource strategy at Rutgers University's School of Management and Labor Relations. Harsh? Yes. But as Huselid points out, "Do you really want C players in your [team] at all?"

In "Debriefing Robert Fritz: Telling the Hard Truth About Poor Performance," business writer Lauren Keller

Johnson interviews Robert Fritz, coauthor with Bruce Bodaken of *The Managerial Moment of Truth: The Essential Step in Helping People Improve Performance*, to get Fritz's thoughts about this particularly difficult aspect of appraising employees' contributions. Fritz lays out a four-step process for delivering critical feedback to an underperformer: (1) Acknowledge the truth by stating the facts related to the poor performance. For example, "The project was due May 23, and now it's May 29." (2) Analyze the employee's thoughts, assumptions, and decisions that led up to the performance failure. (3) With the employee's input, develop an action plan for avoiding similar failures in the future, and ask the person to document the agreed-upon plan in an e-mail or memo. (4) Create a feedback system for tracking progress and addressing any difficulties.

In the final article in this section—"High-Performance Prison"—business writer Jennifer McFarland presents several experts' recommendations for dealing with the unique difficulties of evaluating and managing your star performers. In particular, you'll want to use performance reviews to watch for and address signs of burnout in your best people. For top performers, "success becomes a drug, and [they] constantly feel the need to score." The more they achieve, the greater the risk that they'll experience anxiety over topping their latest success. Managers unwittingly contribute to their stars' anxiety and stress by overloading them with more and more responsibilities—and high performers "will work themselves to death to get [the work] done." The resulting fatigue can eventually reduce these employees' mental capacities, though many of them will strive to conceal the burnout. For these reasons, it's vital to use performance reviews to nip burnout in the bud.

## Understanding the Power of Expectations

As many human resource experts have noted, a performance review is the ideal time to communicate what you expect from employees in the coming period. But conveying expectations effectively requires some care, as the articles in this section make clear. In "Great Expectations: The Key to Great Results?" Lauren Keller Johnson presents experts' and practicing managers' advice for leveraging the power of expectations. Expectations exert a powerful impact on employees' performance—but merely defining and declaring your expectations isn't enough. You also need to apply four practices. For example, involve employees by finding out what they think of the expectations you've presented. People feel more committed to objectives they've helped define—and more confident that they can achieve them. Also discover what each person is most motivated by (competition, close working relationships, variety in their responsibilities). People are most inspired to fulfill expectations that tie into their personal interests.

In "Feedback in the Future Tense," business writer Hal Plotkin argues that communicating clear expectations shifts the performance review from "one primarily about performance—the past—to one about change—the future." Instead of blaming an employee for past mistakes, Plotkin says, "talk quite specifically about how that employee needs to improve. Give the employee a goal to work toward, not a legacy to overcome." Your ultimate goal? "To energize and excite people about the role you need them to play and the development they need to go through" in order to play that role. In addition to clarifying the new behaviors and skills you need employees to demonstrate, use performance evaluations to assess your direct reports' "change capacity" and to "communicate the high value your organization places on a willingness to change and improve." And don't forget to discuss the implications of meeting new expectations—as well as not meeting them.

## Selecting Performance Metrics

To determine whether your employees are delivering good performance, you need to define performance metrics—a major subject in its own right. Of course, employees' metrics depend on their particular job responsibilities. For example, a salesperson's metrics may include "number of new accounts per quarter," while a call center employee's metrics might include "time required to answer a customer's question."

But defining metrics is more complicated than these examples suggest. The most effective metrics take into account not only an employee's job responsibilities and development goals but also the company's high-level objectives. The articles in this section offer guidelines for selecting the right metrics against which to evaluate your subordinates' performance.

In "How to Think About Performance Measures Now," Loren Gary describes a performance management methodology known as the Balanced Scorecard (BSC), developed by Robert Kaplan and David Norton. The BSC enables a company to define the objectives it must achieve in order to carry out its competitive strategy. Those objectives fall into four categories: financial, customer, internal process, and workforce learning and growth. Once an organization has defined high-level objectives and metrics for implementing its strategy, it "cascades" them down business units and departments. Managers then use that information to define individual metrics and targets for their employees that support the high-level goals. For example, the target "10% increase in number of new accounts per quarter by year end" might support a company-level objective of "expanding our customer base." The message? To define performance metrics for your employees, you need to first understand your company's high-level goals.

"Using Measurement to Boost Your Unit's Performance" delves more deeply into this subject by presenting a five-step process for defining unit-level metrics based on company-level goals. For example, one step entails figuring out the performance measures that matter most to your group's ability to support the company's high-level goals. If you're in HR, such numbers might include "average time required to fill a position." If you're in product development, your numbers might include "time to market." By selecting several key unit-level metrics to track, you can more easily translate those into individual metrics for each employee.

In "High-Performance Budgeting," the focus shifts to how you can craft unit-level budgets that support company strategy *and* make use of employees' input. When your direct reports help to create budgets, they feel more motivated to meet or even exceed the agreed-upon goals. And a well-crafted budget establishes a set of specific goals and expectations against which you can compare your people's actual contributions during performance appraisals. To further step up the motivational power of your departmental budget, consider introducing a bonus for hitting agreed-upon targets. If you don't have the authority to offer formal financial rewards, look for nonfinancial forms of reward and recognition instead. Even simply challenging your people to find ways to reduce costs or achieve some other important business goal can motivate them to excel.

In this section's final article—"Of Metrics and Moonbeams: Five Keys to Evaluating the Performance of Knowledge Workers"—business writer Constantine von Hoffman acknowledges the difficulty of selecting performance metrics for employees specializing in knowledge work. For example, while it's easy to determine if a shop-floor worker has produced the desired number of widgets, how do you calculate the level of performance of an employee who is analyzing an industry or market? Von Hoffman provides five tips. For instance, assess performance based on how much employees share knowledge and use one another's ideas. One consulting firm created an electronic repository of knowledge acquired during consulting engagements and began giving employees credit for making "deposits" into the database. Also tailor each performance metric to both your industry and the particular job in question. For example, while "you might judge consultants on the number and depth of relationships they have developed within an industry, you might want analysts to stay as objective as possible and not develop relationships that [could] color their opinions."

## Leveraging 360-Degree Feedback

If you've decided to introduce 360-degree feedback to evaluate your employees' performance, how might you get the most from this controversial tool? The two articles in this section provide ideas. In "Should You Use 360° Feedback for Performance Reviews?" business writer Edward Prewitt conveys experts' tips for applying this tool to formal performance appraisal. Guidelines include introducing 360s purely as an internal tool for individual development and growth before linking it to performance reviews. Explicating the purpose behind using 360s also helps—whether that purpose centers on creating a more open culture or enhancing your performance measurement system. Also make sure that you and others who are using the instrument receive training in how to handle issues such as confidentiality and analysis of data that are gathered.

In "The Ratings Game: Retooling 360s for Better Performance," Lauren Keller Johnson shares additional experts' and practicing managers' thoughts about this tool's promise—and ways to avoid its pitfalls. For example, many executives maintain that successful use of the 360 rests on a foundation of trust and candor. To build a department culture that has these characteristics, consider changing the way you communicate with employees. Instead of avoiding painful conversations and protecting people from troubling news about your unit's performance, make honest announcements about what's going on and what you want your people to do about it. If they don't know what you know about the business, they can't respond by stepping up their performance. Also think about asking 360 survey respondents to augment quantitative ratings with qualitative comments explaining the numerical evaluations they've chosen. Qualitative comments can add a more personal aspect to the feedback and help recipients understand the thinking behind the numbers.

As you read the articles that follow, start thinking about how you might put the ideas and techniques offered here to your own approach to performance assessment. For example:

- Take stock of the process you currently use to evaluate your employees' contributions. To what extent does the process meet the criteria for effectiveness described in the first section of this volume? For example, do you discuss performance on a regular basis with employees throughout the year, or only once? Do you link constructive feedback to important company goals? Do you clarify each direct report's job responsibilities?

- How might you better customize your performance appraisals to meet the unique challenges presented by excellent, average, and poor performers?

- Do you use performance reviews as an opportunity to communicate what you expect from employees in the coming period? If so, do you invite employees' feedback on your expectations, and do you link new expectations to changing goals at the company level?

- What performance metrics have you defined for assessing each employee's contributions? How might you ensure that each metric is appropriate for the job in question, and that each metric supports unit- and company-level objectives?

- Do you currently use 360-degree feedback as part of your performance appraisal process? If so, what benefits have you obtained from using this tool? What difficulties have you encountered? What steps might you take to address the difficulties and enhance the benefits?

# Maximizing Your Performance Management System

• • •

The most effective performance appraisal systems exhibit certain shared characteristics—such as ongoing, two-way exchanges of feedback; regular coaching between manager and employee; separation of conversations devoted to professional development and compensation decisions; and explicit links between performance goals and high-level company objectives.

In the articles that make up this section, you'll learn more about these characteristics and discover ways to ensure that your own performance appraisal approach demonstrates them. The section concludes with a checklist you can use to further evaluate the effectiveness of your approach and to make changes if needed.

# Performance Appraisal Is Dead. Long Live Performance Management!

. . .

Monci J. Williams

Next to receiving his superior's assessment of his own performance, the most dreaded moments in a manager's life may be those in which he delivers a performance appraisal to someone else. And no wonder. At its worst, a performance appraisal is nothing more than a report card given by a boss to a subordinate, a verdict on professional adequacy or the lack of it. The performance appraisal's message, no matter how sliced, diced, or hidden under leafy garnishes, always boils down to "Here's what's wrong with you." Only the most sadistic among us could enjoy serving up such fare to the squirming customer on the other side of the desk.

Or take another common scenario: Hours of preparation and piles of paper, each multiplied by the number of people reporting to the manager doing the appraisals, culminate in a series of wooden exercises in which what is not said looms largest, no one suffers much discomfort, and nothing worthwhile is accomplished. It's a drill more like a scene out of *Dr. Strangelove* or *Catch-22* than a well-managed, moving-into-the-new-millennium enterprise.

It was inevitable, then, given progress in how business treats people, that management experts would wake up to the inadequacy of the traditional performance appraisal. And so they did, starting some ten years ago. Executives hard-pressed for results, and the consultants pressed to help them achieve results, saw what the rest of us have known for years: by themselves, old-style performance appraisals are neither as useful to the individual nor as effective in helping the corporation reach its goals as they should be.

Specialists at firms like Personnel Decisions International, a human resource consulting and training firm, and Development Directions International, a consulting and training company, as well as increasing numbers of HR and operating executives, now refer to the performance appraisal and the one-way feedback it provides as "archaic," a "relic" of an industrial-based management system whose effectiveness has been outmoded by new competitive imperatives and changing employee expectations.

So forget performance appraisal, and think—slight blare of trumpets here, heralding an innovation—performance management. While the former is largely a one-time, one-way report card, performance management is a two-way, continuous process of observation, conversation, thinking, planning, and coaching that occurs throughout the year. The good word from the experts is that by managing performance instead of just performing appraisals, companies can improve employee performance—and hence corporate performance—along with saving managers considerable time and angst. Managers who have tried the new system agree.

## Performance Management: The Theory

While appraisal of an employee's efforts remains a fundamental part of performance management, it is appraisal with what the experts call an empowering, rather than a merely evaluative, end in mind. Performance management integrates appraisal of employees' performance with two-way feedback, development, and goalsetting. And while human resource and compensation experts have been working for years to link the evaluation and compensation of senior executives to corporate performance, the latest performance management systems tie appraisal, development, and goalsetting to the financial and strategic goals of the corporation for all employees.

The most important new wrinkle is the extent to which these new systems, which are in place at a growing number of companies, can, in effect, "engineer" the behavior of employees. In leading-edge systems, companies don't just talk about lofty missions or strategic aims such as customer satisfaction and market leadership. They define the specific behaviors that embody these goals, communicate them to employees, and "appraise" their performance on those behaviors as well as their achievement of numerical targets.

In these systems, appraisal is not the end but a kind of beginning. Managers work with employees to identify both skill deficits and new skills that the company may require of its workers in the years ahead. With help along these lines, the employee puts together a plan for her own development and training that will enable her to master the desired behaviors.

## Performance Management: The Practice

At The Limited, a $10 billion-a-year retail company that has 14 different retail businesses and five nonretailing operations, a new performance management system instituted two years ago replaced one in which employees were evaluated only on whether they hit quantitative targets. The company, says Bob Myers, vice president of organizational and leadership development, was at a critical turning point and had no way to ensure that its managers were developing the needed skills to help the company meet present and future challenges. Long a decentralized organization that gave free rein to each operating unit, The Limited was entering a period of consolidation in which managers would be made more accountable for contributions to broader corporate goals. Yet it did not want to sacrifice the entrepreneurial drive that had been key to its success.

Working with Personnel Decisions, The Limited identified 19 competencies it wanted its managers to demonstrate, among them strategic thinking, planning, and execution. The result of instituting a system in which they were measured against their progress on those dimensions, says Myers, has been an improvement in individual performance, and for a very simple reason: "People's performance is better because people are better directed."

Managers in the Greenville Hospital System in South Carolina, which instituted a new integrated performance management system designed by DDI two years ago, have seen similar results. Driven to control costs as hospitals in its region consolidated, the Greenville Hospital System replaced its performance appraisal process with one that defines "dimensions"—specific behaviors by employees that the company believes will help it accomplish its objectives.

In addition to cost control, the objectives include high-quality customer service, collaboration, and initiative. Specific behaviors are assigned various weightings tied to the company's strategic objectives. The new system also includes an element that may be of great interest to managers drowning in paperwork, reports, and e-mail. Employees—not managers—log and report their own performance of required behaviors.

Jack Macauley, executive director of materials management for the hospital system, says that linking performance appraisals and individual employees' priorities to those of the corporation has made cost control easier to achieve. "To control costs, purchasing has to work with the clinicians, and vice versa. No one individual can do it alone. Performance management drives everyone toward interdisciplinary cooperation and a team effort."

## The Critical Application: Having Those Conversations

In truth, managers who seek to influence the performance of their employees need not always have the support of an elaborate corporate system. The most effective performance management approaches build on long-standing practices that were effective as far as they went—which wasn't quite far enough—and simply take them further. Most important, these new approaches provide detailed tactics for the most basic, most difficult, and most critical part of performance management—how to talk to the employee.

## Let your motto be: all talk, all the time.

The critical "how" of performance management is, in fact, a "when." The phrase long in use by performance experts has been "continuous conversation." Advocates of the new performance management systems suggest that managers have three or four performance-related conversations with each direct report in the course of the year. Minimally, performance "appraisal"—i.e., a review of progress toward previously defined, measurable goals—should be part of each of these discussions, rather than being accumulated for one dreaded session at year-end.

Continuous feedback gives the employee the opportunity to adjust behavior as he or she goes along. "An employee can operate more like a guided missile, which adjusts course as needed," argues Jane Schenck, a principal of Catalyst Systems, a human resource consulting firm. Says Thomas Wester, vice president of operations for Peoples Natural Gas, "Performance appraisal is not an event. It's not discrete, and it's not confined to the formal procedure required by my company. The real work is what comes in between."

## Communicate expectations.

"A lack of communication means that employees will fill in the blanks on their own," observes Wester. But there's a lot of ground between the reasonable expectation that an employee act like a mature member of the team and the expectation that he or she will read your mind. Accordingly, says Wester, "The role of the supervisor is to communicate the expectations and the reasons for them."

In this regard, there is an important distinction between feedback and real communication. Feedback is most often practiced as a one-way data dump and will likely engender defensiveness. Says David Peterson of Personnel Decisions, "Feedback may communicate information on past performance, but it doesn't traditionally include information about expectations. And so it doesn't contribute to insight."

Communicating expectations can be particularly important, and effective, to someone whose role is changing—for example, when a product manager moves up to general manager: "We see you're a great team leader, good at getting things out on time and managing costs. Now we need you to drive the business—focus on the whole financial picture, think about where the profits will come from."

## Positive feedback is a necessary emolument.

Industrial psychologists (as well as marriage counselors) say people handle criticism best when it is delivered in a ratio of one to three—one criticism for every three compliments.

## Link comments about past performance to future goals.

Employees can't change the past. They *can* influence what they do from now on. So the most effective stance in a conversation with an employee is a focus on the constructive action that can be taken in the future. "If we didn't achieve X, let's look at why. Were the goals unrealistic? Were there additional skills lacking that we can build into your developmental plan for the year ahead?"

## Stop being the boss.

Start being the coach. Notice the use of the inclusive "we" in the example above. The best way to ensure that an employee will not be defensive or resistant to your comments, says Peterson of Personnel Decisions, is to "forge a partnership" that makes coaching an unremarkable element of the manager's relationship with the employee.

Personnel Decisions consultants train their clients to be alert to "coachable moments," those events that give the manager an opportunity to lay a little wisdom on the employee.

Indeed, performance management is about more than conversation—it's about the manager's attitude, his stance. Wester says he thinks in terms of relationship, and practices performance management as part of the warp and woof of his relationships with direct reports. "Performance management," like coaching in sports, "is an art," he says.

### Focus on behavior, not personality.

Say, for example, that one of your reports is hypothetical Sally, a technical wizard who is a bit insecure, needs to feel superior, and tries to demonstrate superiority by showing the world that she's smarter than her colleagues. In a recent meeting, she interrupted Joe and corrected him.

> Be alert to "coachable moments," those events that give the manager an opportunity to lay a little wisdom on the employee.

In the first "coachable moment" after the meeting, the manager can draw Sally's attention to the exchange. Rather than observe that she is obnoxious, arrogant, or irritating—or simply shun her—Sally's manager should simply ask her: "Were you aware that you interrupted Joe and corrected him?"

## Help the employee focus on the desirable, or undesirable, result of a behavior.

Continuous feedback includes reinforcing employees who exhibit the behaviors the company believes will help it achieve its business goals. And so the manager is charged with saying to an employee, "You showed initiative in the way you handled a customer complaint by arranging for the product to be shipped back to us at no charge to the customer."

At Sally's company, the manager might ask: "How do you think that made Joe and everyone else feel?" The manager might also observe that people tend to shun know-it-alls, and that if Sally repeats the behavior she might find it hard to move up in the company or out of it.

Consultants at PDI call this "making feedback relevant," but Wester says it's only common sense. "Everybody views the world from a different frame of reference," he says, so find their frame and use it. Wester might continue his conversation with Sally by asking her what her career goals are, or how she wants to be viewed. "I want to be seen as the most technically competent person in my area," she might respond. "Well," Wester might answer, "I think you're on that track. But my question to you is: At what cost?"

## Separate conversations about development from conversations about compensation.

One conversation looks forward; the other looks back. One is about future value to the company; one about current. "There's too much information to digest in each one," says Bob Myers of The Limited. Moreover, it's tough for employees to concentrate on next year's developmental goals when they're thinking about the size of their raise—or the absence of one.

## Examine your own biases and eliminate them from performance conversations.

Wester likes to use anecdotes to communicate with employees, and one involving himself might be most instructive here. He was having a performance conversation with an employee in which he outlined his expectations. The employee, says Wester, "implied those standards might be a little high. I gave him the standard supervisor's response: 'I'm not asking you to do anything I wouldn't do.' And the employee said, 'You're right. But you drive yourself like a son of a bitch.'"

Wester learned from the exchange to challenge himself on his expectations for other people. "The expectations for performance have to be based on the company's business needs and the scope of the job description." Period.

## So What's a Manager for?

Companies achieve results not by poring over numbers, but by poring over the people who do the things that make the numbers what they are. That means a manager must get closer to his employees—and take more responsibility for the performance of each one—than ever before.

Doing so may be a bit discomfiting if you're a graduate of one of the schools of management science that implicitly encouraged you to handle employees with all the enthusiasm of a latex-gloved research scientist meeting up with a Petri dish. But there is no other way to translate business goals into desired human behaviors, the core job of the manager. And since, as managers, we can't achieve results without people, we might as well learn to live with them, do what we can to help them do the right thing, and love it.

**Reprint U9702A**

# Alternatives to Performance Reviews

. . .

At most companies, performance reviews are as popular as root canals. Abolish them, you might think, and managers and employees alike would breathe a collective sigh of relief. But then what would happen to motivation, merit-pay differentials, even performance itself—all those things that reviews are supposed to drive or inform?

This is a debate that has rumbled along quietly for years now, both in HR circles and in executive suites. On the one hand, companies are sorely tempted to eliminate reviews completely. Because people regard them with so much fear and loathing, they're postponed, gamed, glossed over, and generally viewed as something to be survived rather than used. Moreover, critics argue persuasively that reviews fail to accomplish their ostensible purposes and succeed only in demoralizing and demotivating employees.

On the other hand are all those nagging concerns. If managers aren't required to give feedback, they may not do so at all. Employees' motivation and personal development will suffer. Performance will decline. The company will have no basis for awarding pay increases and no paper trail to cover itself if an employee must be let go.

What's the solution? Some companies actually have abolished annual reviews. But it isn't an easy move to make. Managers have to change some fundamental assumptions about what really produces high performance, and companies have to work with employees differently on a variety of fronts, from feedback to compensation.

## The Case Against Reviews

The issue wouldn't arise if performance appraisals weren't so fraught with difficulties. Part of the problem is that people on both sides of the desk hate the process and therefore find ways to manipulate or avoid it. But even in the best of circumstances, reviews may not accomplish their objectives. Consider just a few of the critics' charges:

## Managers can't assess employees' performance accurately.

Everybody can recognize a true superstar or a world-class slacker. But how many managers can accurately judge the performance of 10 or 20 direct reports, most of whom are in the broad middle range and probably doing as good a job as their tools, training, and work environment allow? Attempts to hand out individual ratings are inevitably colored by personality, emotion, and selective memory.

## Formal evaluations demotivate more than they motivate.

If a performance-review system hands out high marks to all, it's a charade that no one will take seriously. To prevent rate inflation of this sort, many companies require managers to grade employees on a curve and hand out merit-pay increases accordingly. Now the company has another problem: the losers may be little different in outlook or performance from the winners, but there's no doubt in anyone's mind that they have been dubbed losers. "In the span of a 30-minute meeting, [a review] can transform a vibrant, highly committed employee into a demoralized, indifferent wallflower who reads the want-ads on the weekend," write Tom Coens and Mary Jenkins in their book *Abolishing Performance Appraisals: Why They Backfire and What to Do Instead.*

## Reviews don't improve firm performance.

Reviews examine what individuals do and (in theory) motivate them to do better. But individual performance is seldom the key to better organizational performance. "Most problems, and therefore most opportunities for improvement, are in your systems and processes, not in your individuals and groups," argues Peter R. Scholtes, author of *Total Quality Versus Performance Appraisal, Choose One*, who has been in the vanguard of attacks on annual reviews. Scholtes—reflecting the thinking of the late W. Edwards Deming—assumes that most people want to do a good job and are constrained in their efforts by poorly designed systems or work environments. His conclusions? Fix the system, not the people. Judge performance by the output of work groups and business units, not by the efforts exerted by individuals.

Over the years, companies have monkeyed with the review process—for example, by asking employees to establish goals and using those as the basis for the review. Critics such as Coens and Jenkins cast a jaundiced eye on these reforms as well. If people don't accomplish their goals, they ask, is that their fault, or did something about "the system in which they work" impede them? If people do accomplish their written goals, have they unwittingly sacrificed other objectives? Have they blindly stuck to what they decided on six or nine months ago, rather than adapting their behavior to what's needed now?

# The Alternative: Unbundling

What keeps performance reviews alive is a combination of hope and despair: hope that reviews will somehow accomplish their objectives despite the odds, despair over the difficulty of accomplishing those objectives any other way. But a handful of companies have done just what the critics recommend, which is to unbundle these functions and create separate methods for achieving the desired results. Some examples of this approach:

## Feedback

Reviews are meant to provide feedback so that employees can learn from mistakes and build on their strengths. The objective is valid, but the tool is problematic. Reviews offer feedback only once or twice a year. The feedback is initiated by the boss (or by HR), focuses entirely on the individual, goes into the personnel file, and may be tied directly to a raise. The system thus provides every incentive for employees to make themselves look good and for kindhearted managers to overlook mistakes.

Companies that have abolished performance reviews approach feedback differently. SAS Institute, a software firm, encourages each division to design its own feedback procedures but expects that some kind of discussion between employees and managers will take place at least monthly. No one is rated, says HR project manager Annette Holesh, and nothing goes in the file unless the employee requests it. Wheaton Franciscan Services, a health care and housing company, holds feedback sessions that focus on "the working relationship between

> What keeps performance reviews alive is a combination of hope and despair.

the employee and the system within which they work," says former Wheaton SVP Bob Strickland. The purpose of these sessions isn't to assess an individual's performance; rather, manager and employee use the session "to identify where improvements could be made and then to plan those improvements," says Strickland.

## Merit Pay

Performance reviews at many companies provide both the basis for determining raises and a forum for discussing them with employees. This is not a marriage made in heaven: if money is on the agenda, everything else invariably dwindles in importance. But there's a more fundamental problem with linking appraisals to pay, which is that the two may not correlate. "If you have wages based on performance reviews, and you have a tight lid on raises," one HR expert recently pointed out in the magazine *Nation's Business*, "it means your performance reviews can't be very good."

Deming aficionados and other performance-review critics tend to be critical of merit pay itself. So most of the companies that have eliminated reviews have also created different procedures for determining raises. General Motors' powertrain division awards pay increases based on an employee's experience within a given pay grade. Some companies award raises to employees who acquire specific new skills. SAS does offer merit-based raises but handles the pay process separately from the feedback system.

## Legal Cover

Reviews provide a paper trail of an individual's performance; when an employee must be dismissed, the record offers protection against lawsuits, or so goes the theory. In fact, experts say, a broad-based performance-appraisal system is an ineffective means to this end. Reviews are infrequent. The language contained in them is often ambiguous. Most companies' records exhibit inconsistencies that a skilled lawyer can pick apart easily in court.

A better alternative may be a special evaluation system designed only for the tiny minority of employees who risk dismissal. Scholtes favors performance appraisal "as a temporary intervention with an employee whose work is outstandingly poor, to remove any possible ambiguity regarding short-term expectations."

This isn't a complete list of the problems posed by abolishing performance reviews. Companies must also come up with alternative ways to identify candidates for promotion. They must ascertain employees' training needs and make sure that people are encouraged to take advantage of skill-building opportunities. These and other tasks ensure that eliminating reviews is a challenging undertaking.

Is it worth it? Many companies will decide it isn't. But some may find that abolishing reviews forces them to think about management practices they take for granted. They also may find that it cuts down on turnover, simply because both managers and employees like the new practices better than the old.

**Reprint U0606D**

# Performance Appraisals with More Gain, Less Pain

• • •

Peter L. Allen

Short of firing, what is the responsibility managers hate the most? If you're thinking "performance appraisal," then you may have something to learn from *The Performance Appraisal Question and Answer Book: A Survival Guide for Managers*, by Dick Grote, a former manager at General Electric and PepsiCo who has become one of the country's leading experts on the topic. While this practical handbook may not make you look forward to your next set of year-end meetings, it can certainly help you manage the process far more effectively—and spare you that "I'd really rather be having a root canal" feeling into the bargain.

Performance appraisal, if done correctly, says Grote, can become the most valuable instrument in the manager's toolbox. "No other management process," he says, "has as much influence over individuals' careers and work lives." Let's consider the benefits. On the most practical level, the few hours a manager invests in a careful appraisal process can help improve an employee's performance for an entire year. More broadly, an effective evaluation process is part of the strategic first-rate people management that helps top companies succeed. In fact, many of the companies judged the best at performance evaluation in a 1999 survey conducted by the American Productivity & Quality Center and Linkage Inc. refused to divulge their evaluation techniques, viewing them as key components of their competitive strategies. "We would no more show our performance appraisal form to a bunch of outsiders," said one participating VP of human resources, "than the Coca-Cola Company would let you come in and look over the secret formula for Coke."

## The Calendar, Not the Clock

A successful performance appraisal process rests on a few key fundamentals: timing, clarity, and consistency.

Timing first. Performance appraisals should be governed by the calendar, not the clock. Managers should hold at least two formal meetings with each employee every year—one at the beginning, to plan, and one at the end, to review. And in between, managers should be coaching their employees every day.

They should also keep a regular written log of employees' performance. Why a log? Because managers, being human, have imperfect memories. Many people in supervisory roles don't prepare for evaluations until the very end of the year that the reviews are supposed to evaluate. Between recency bias and the all-too-human tendency to focus on the negative, however, a December retrospective is likely to lose track of many examples of positive performance from the previous 11 months. ("There are no such things," warns Grote, "as mental notes.") Lesson: Start early.

Clear understanding of the position in question comes next: You can't evaluate how well an employee has done a job until both of you are clear about exactly what the job is. Every position, says Grote, has five or six key responsibilities. If you didn't clearly articulate them earlier in the year, you need to sit down and figure them out before you start evaluating how well the employee has handled them.

Item three is consistency. A truly effective review process, Grote reminds his readers, is one that ties directly into the company's mission statement and values. This principle may seem head-thumpingly obvious, but in practice it's as rare as a consultant without a cell

phone. Case in point: An informal survey Grote conducted several years ago, when speaking before a group
of human resources executives from many of the companies in the Fortune 1000.

> "How many of you," he asked, "can take your
> performance appraisal form in your left hand and
> your mission statement in your right hand, and walk
> up to one of your employees and say, 'Harry, look!
> Do you see where the words in the performance
> appraisal and the words in the mission statement
> are the same words?' If you can, raise your hand."

Of the 600 right hands in the room, only about 19
went up. Would yours?

## Brass Tacks

Grote's pragmatic Q&A format focuses on the practical
details as much as it does on general principles. How, for
instance, can your company phrase the questions in its
appraisal form so that managers can evaluate their staff
accurately without raising hackles? One suggestion:
Solicit facts, not opinions. Don't ask, "How good was
this employee's performance?" Instead, ask, "What proportion of the time did the employee perform this task
at a truly professional level?" The more objective the
questions, the more useful and persuasive the answers
will be.

Another practical insight: Evaluation inflation, and employees' expectations of inflated ratings, can be avoided by pegging the score range in the right place. According to the laws of mathematics, most people do an average job. According to the laws of human nature, however, most people hate to be rated as average.

If you have a five-point evaluation scale, then, don't characterize the middle rating as "acceptable" or "fair." Instead, treat it as a "par" score in golf. Par, Grote

> Eliciting peak performance begins with designing satisfying jobs but doesn't end there.

reminds us, "doesn't mean average or mediocre. . . . A pro golfer can often do better, but par is what is expected of an expert." If reaching the middle score is an accomplishment people can be proud of, a company can reset inflated expectations and get a valid read on performance as well.

Grote also recommends that senior HR managers who supervise the company's evaluation process train managers to fill out evaluation forms correctly and calibrate scores for consistency across the organization.

*The Performance Appraisal Question and Answer Book* also offers advice on how to handle the dreaded review meeting. Some suggestions are simple tips that too many managers fail to follow. Be brave enough to tell the truth, and rest your case on specific examples when you do. Avoid surprises. And if you want to be heard, don't just talk—listen, too.

One last practical tip: As you prepare for the review meeting, focus. People rarely hear everything you say, particularly when they are ill at ease or under stress. So if you want the employee to hear a core message, make it clear to yourself first. Grote says:

> Imagine that a few weeks ago you had your annual
> performance appraisal discussion with Joanne.
> This morning, as you're walking down the
> hall, . . . you pull her aside and say, 'Joanne, a few
> weeks ago we had a performance appraisal
> discussion. Tell me something . . . what do you
> remember from that discussion?' What is that one
> thing that you want to have stuck in her memory?
> Whatever it is, that is your core message.

## Set Goals and Achieve Them

Performance appraisal is a tool to facilitate good management—a means to an end, not an end in itself. With this idea in mind, Grote bases the performance appraisal process on the principle (set forth long ago by Peter Drucker) that the best managers help their people do two main things: Set goals and achieve them.

Douglas McGregor expounded upon this theory in the *Harvard Business Review* back in 1957. Developing people effectively, he argued in the language of the era,

> . . . does not include coercing them (no matter how benevolently) into acceptance of the goals of the enterprise, nor does it mean manipulating their behavior to suit organizational needs. Rather, it calls for creating a relationship within which a man can take responsibility for developing his own potentialities, plan for himself, and learn from putting his plan into action.

This theory underlies the success that performance appraisal is designed to measure.

Soon after Drucker and McGregor articulated the principle of management by objectives, General Electric studied its implications. "Criticism," GE found, "has a negative effect on achievement of goals; praise has little effect one way or the other." GE also determined that the best way to improve performance is to have manager and employee sit down together and establish specific goals that are based on the individual's strengths. This approach beats relying only on such secondary stimuli as good salaries, generous benefits packages, job security, or prestige. Why? Because real job satisfaction, commitment, and a sense of achievement come ultimately from the job itself.

Eliciting peak performance begins with designing satisfying jobs but doesn't end there. You have to find the best people to fill these positions; plan employees' daily, monthly, and yearly tasks; create conditions that motivate; and deal with problems as they come up. Evaluating the work that has been done, though an important step, comes only at the end of the process. Managers who do all of these steps right will find that performance appraisal is no longer an ordeal they dread, but rather a valuable tool that helps them do their own jobs better—namely, helping their employees do the best job they can.

**Reprint C0303D**

# Successful Performance Measurement

## A Checklist

• • •

**Karen Carney**

Rare is the company that doesn't sport some kind of performance-measurement program. Organizations of all sorts track and assess the output of business units, departments, managers, even individual employees. They benchmark performance against preestablished goals; they pay bonuses to employees or units who reach their objectives.

But *successful* measurement systems—systems that energize employees and so actually do what they're supposed to do, which is boost performance—are harder to find. Too often, employees don't buy into the system, so it doesn't affect their behavior. If they get a bonus for reaching some objective they don't understand or haven't worked toward, the extra money just seems like a random reward.

How does your own company's system stack up? Do a little performance measurement of your own: assess it against this checklist.

## Our system starts with big-picture goals—and everyone knows what they are.

Any manager can set performance goals for work groups or individuals, but those immediate targets will always seem arbitrary unless people understand how they tie into big-picture objectives. Does your company or business unit have clear, well-understood objectives? Are they widely publicized?

At United Ad Label (UAL), a label manufacturer for the health-care industry, the leadership team held a three-day retreat last year to develop a "Y2K balanced scorecard" spelling out the company's overall business strategy and mission, with supporting objectives in key areas such as business processes and marketplace

51

presence. A separate scorecard spells out numerical goals related to performance in each area. For example, UAL wants X% of sales to come from new products and markets by the close of 1999. It wants Y new strategic alliances in place. It has targets for EBIT/sales and

> # One powerful tool: "scoreboards" on the wall—or on people's computer screens.

return on capital. These objectives are posted around the company's facility for all to see. "Knowing what we're trying to accomplish as a company helps people at every level make more informed decisions everyday," says Valerie Poole, manager of human resources.

## Every group has performance drivers linked to the big-picture objectives.

How do people's jobs tie in to those overall goals? Usually departments need specific objectives that are tied to the company's. Given a certain growth target and historical data about turnover, for instance, an HR department should know how many new hires it will be responsible for—and should assess its performance in delivering these new people in a timely fashion.

At UAL, shop-floor employees focus on reducing cycle time and minimizing returns and allowances, both of which affect operating income. ("We do custom work, and if we don't get it right the first time or if the shipment arrives late, we know it's going to cost us," says Poole.) Customer-service team members know that to reach the company's market-share objectives, they'll need reorders from 70% of existing customers. They monitor not just that number but all the activities that contribute to it, such as customer satisfaction rates, abandoned-call rates, and on-time mailing of brochures.

## Individual and work-group performance objectives are clear—and reasonable.

Targets for performance can be set in units shipped, dollars of revenue or expense, defect rates, customer satisfaction rates, or any other metric that makes sense. In some cases, job-specific goals—meetings held with customers, calls answered by the second ring—can be helpful, so long as the individuals involved are also part of a group with larger objectives. Even people whose work isn't easily quantifiable should be held accountable for

## Measuring the Soft Stuff

What about "soft" metrics—measurement and assessment of work that doesn't lend itself to easy quantification? There are three keys to effective performance measurement of this kind of job:

1. Involve people in determining their own measurement criteria.

Jack Zigon of Zigon Performance Group suggests several methods. Ask them, "If you weren't on this team, what wouldn't get done?" Hand out a list of unit or company goals and ask them which ones they can affect. Get people brainstorming about who their internal and external customers are, and what they can do to delight these customers. Nearly all work can be evaluated using a combination of descriptive terms and behavioral objectives. An IT service technician, for instance, can be prompt and friendly or slow and abrasive in delivering assistance. A marketing team can be imaginative and creative or uninspired and stodgy.

2. Find qualified judges to assess people's performance according to these criteria.

performance objectives. If the performance targets aren't reasonable or are perceived as unfair, of course, employees will dismiss them out of hand. On the other hand, you may want to develop stretch goals for the quarter or the year in case your unit blows past the "reasonable" targets.

Judges can be employees, customers, suppliers, business partners, or anyone else who can determine if a result or behavior meets, exceeds, or falls short of expectations. As in diving or figure skating, it's the judges' ratings that gauge performance.

3. Combine hard and soft metrics as appropriate.

At McMurry Publishing, associates receive generous bonuses based on the bottom-line results of their business units. Salary increases, however, are based on assessments of behavior. Once a year, managers endure a four-hour performance evaluation that rates them on how fully they embody McMurry's eight core values (among them: *does the right thing, delivers raving customer service,* and *always produces quality*) and how well they use those values to guide associates. Raters are encouraged to talk with at least five people who work closely with the manager being reviewed. Subsequently, managers score associates on a scale of 1 to 5 on how well they follow key operating strategies, such as *makes decisions quickly, accepts responsibility,* and *pursues growth aggressively.* The entire process and the relevant measurements are spelled out in McMurry's employee handbook.

## We educate and coach employees continually.

It happens often: companies launch a performance-measurement system with plenty of hoopla and plenty of training. A year later, employees have forgotten what

55

most of the measurements mean—and new employees are utterly mystified. A particularly important task: communicating the connections between work-group and big-picture goals, which in large companies are likely to be obscure. Leaders at Amoco Canada, for example, make a point of taking business units' income statements and showing each job group—engineering, finance, administration, operations, and so on—the costs they can control and how they can affect different facets of the overall financial goals. "If you say to them, 'Look, that vehicle cost number ties into our area number, which ties into our total operations number,' then people can really start to see that cascading effect of the numbers," says Fred Plummer, progress coordinator for Amoco's liquids business unit. "And, more important, how they can make a difference."

## We have a clear and simple system that tracks progress toward our goals.

Most companies have well-developed systems for tracking financial performance, but not many have equally sophisticated methods of tracking progress in customer satisfaction, time-to-market, or other strategically important objectives. What is tracked, of course, must be communicated in such a way that employees see and can follow the results. One powerful tool: "scoreboards" that are literally on office walls or employees' computer screens.

At Civco Medical Instruments, for example, the primary scoreboard is an abbreviated income statement that shows the company's sales-and-expense figures by month and by year-to-date, both compared to plan. The figures, which are updated weekly and projected out six months, are posted throughout the company's facilities for all to see. Companion scorecards detail line-by-line expenses related to sales and marketing, G&A, and product development. Other graphs and charts illustrate trends in key metrics such as historical and projected sales by customer, international sales, incentive-compensation results, and telemarketing efforts.

---

### For Further Reading

*The Balanced Scorecard: Translating Strategy into Action* by Robert S. Kaplan and David P. Norton (1996, Harvard Business School Press)

*Balanced Scorecard Report,* a bimonthly newsletter published by Harvard Business School and The Balanced Scorecard Collaborative (800-668-6705 or [outside the U.S.] 617-783-7474)

*Make Success Measurable: A Mindbook-Workbook for Setting Goals and Taking Action* by Douglas K. Smith (1999, John Wiley & Sons)

**Reprint U9911B**

# Handling Excellent, Average, and Poor Performers

· · ·

Many managers find it easy to recognize a true superstar or a world-class slacker. But how can you be certain you're accurately judging the contributions of 10, 20, or more direct reports—most of whom fall into the broad range between star and slacker and who are probably performing as well as their training, tools, and work environment allow?

It's important to customize your performance reviews for top talent, average contributors, and poor performers. But how, precisely, should you tailor your feedback for each of these employee categories? The articles that follow provide helpful guidance so you can leverage star performers' abilities and bring average performance up a notch or two—as well as address inadequate on-the-job contributions.

# How to Get the Best Out of Performance Reviews

•  •  •

**Michael E. Hattersley**

It's Tuesday morning, and you're facing the second toughest challenge in a manager's job description, almost as bad as handing someone a pink slip. It's the day you do the annual performance review for your team—and you have to deliver the forms by 5 p.m. To make matters worse, the first employee up is a problem case. He's not a team player, and displays a lot of bad attitude—but he has extraordinary bouts of creativity that have been important to the department's success. What do you say to get him to improve?

Most organizations mandate periodic reviews and more or less dictate the format. The process often requires a manager to give bad or mixed news to a colleague, or even a friend. Following some rules based on research, experience, and common sense can help ensure that performance reviews actually result in better performance.

Keep in mind that people perform well or badly in their jobs not only by virtue of intelligence or training, but also according to personality. No rules can govern how to interpret the infinite variety of human behavior and relationships, but the effective manager will keep track of—and factor into job assignments—an understanding of how each personality fits the task, and which employees can work together well. Not all can.

> A good performance review is an ongoing process rather than a one-time event.

Also, when preparing to give a performance review, look at how this particular subordinate fits into the big picture. It's a good opportunity for the manager to consider the general staffing situation: whether the right people are doing the right jobs. Perhaps the person you're about to upset with a bad review might be excellent in another position. Ask yourself: Does he have the capacity to improve? Is he in the right job, or are there creative opportunities to redistribute workload so everyone is doing what inspires them most? Is this someone who's doing his adequate best in a necessary position, and should I leave well enough alone?

## Different Approaches at Different Companies

Priscilla King, human resources director for information systems and services at General Motors, has some advice. First, she distinguishes between more traditional corporations, which help people adjust to the organization, and flatter corporations, which believe in turnover and tend to fire the bottom 10% of performers every year. In the first case, the human resources department plays a significant role in molding the right person to the right job. In the second, you're on your own.

At GM, performance reviews are conducted annually. Reviewers work from a written form. First, they identify the goals for the employee and stress how the boss will help them improve. Then they move to developmental objectives, including training, new assignments, new projects, and career planning. The review includes an assessment of how well the employee has met goals established at the last session.

King believes that a proactive human resources department, or its equivalent, is crucial to getting the best performance out of employees. GM's human resources department maintains an "open door policy" for both the reviewers and the reviewed. Sometimes supervisors come to HR and say, "This is a very talented person but she belongs somewhere else." In that case, HR, the boss, and the employee will work together to find a position that better suits the talent, although this task is ultimately the employee's responsibility. Sometimes, employees dispute their reviews, in which case HR offers counseling to both sides and tries to see the review through to a mutually acceptable conclusion.

King's advice: "Overcommunicate. You can never communicate enough."

## Does Anyone Really Want the Truth?

Robert Kent, who headed the management communication course at Harvard Business School, takes a more provocative approach to performance reviews. He starts by quoting the novelist Somerset Maugham: "People ask you for criticism, but they only want praise." Kent suggests working the following questions into the interview:

- Are you happy here?

- Do you want to stay?

- Are you working hard enough?

- Are you getting enough play time?

- Are you satisfied with your compensation?

- Are you looking for promotion?

- Do you appreciate your peers?

- Do you feel they appreciate you?

Kent recommends, if your organization's policies allow it, raising these issues, then giving the subordinate a week to think about them before coming back for a follow-up interview.

Bob Braun of Braun Consulting Group, which advises firms large and small on employee relations policies, recommends that where evaluations have become routine or are not rigorously monitored, they should be discontinued. His reason: "Overly generous evaluations can come back to haunt the employer."

Braun suggests beginning the review with a self-evaluation form, and cites three reasons why this is the best approach. First, employees will often identify performance problems and this sets up the supervisor as a coach rather than a disciplinarian. Second, this approach helps identify how the supervisor and the employee see performance differently. Finally, says Braun, "The lower-paid employee, not the supervisor, spends the most time on documentation." Braun emphasizes that each review must result in an action plan. He also recommends that the final product go to the supervisor's boss for approval, so as to monitor the supervisor's review skills. Braun concludes, "The goal of the evaluation process

> ## Nothing in the performance review should come as a surprise.

should be to improve collective performance one individual at a time." He adds, "Don't talk about penalties for failure, talk about rewards for success."

## Rules for Well-Conducted Reviews

Prepare for the review by assessing the subordinate's capacity to improve. One employee of very average talents may be working hard and cooperatively, while another brilliant colleague is a difficult slacker.

Nothing in the performance review should come as a surprise. What this really means is that a good performance review is an ongoing process rather than a one-time event. Effective feedback has to be continuous—"Good speech," or "I thought you were a little hostile at the meeting today," or "You seem to be frustrated about X; let's talk about it." Lack of surprise may be the most important single factor in successful performance reviews.

Try not to rely on hearsay. Instead, rely on direct observation and objective data. There are times when it may be necessary to say something like "Everyone who's ever worked with you says they have the same problem."

Provide individual resources to fix any problems you've identified. Resources of training, developmental counseling, job placement, and so forth will, of course, vary dramatically from one organization to another. Ongoing resources that don't single out the individual as a problem can be helpful. This can include skills or communication training. Sometimes the help the person needs—from a community college course to a marriage counselor—exists outside the organization. But unless you've decided to fire the employee, be prepared to demonstrate that you're doing everything you can.

You may need to conduct three kinds of reviews, for poor, average, or top performers.

## Handling the Poor Performer

This is the toughest situation. If you can do a good job of a bad performance review, the others will come easy.

If the performance is bad, say so right away but hold out some hope for improvement. Be as specific as you can about what's wrong and how it can be fixed. You'll have established objective criteria if you have to fire the employee next time.

Avoid the "you're one, too" trap. Often subordinates will respond to criticism with the charge that the reviewer or another colleague has the same faults. Don't get drawn into an argument. Instead, point out that you'll be reviewed too, but that this session is about the subordinate.

Be prepared to describe the appeal process, if there is one. If your company has an HR department, you may want to get its advice in advance of the review.

Defuse the review as much as possible. Stick to clear performance criteria rather than attack the subordinate's personality, which isn't likely to change.

## Coping with the Average Performer

All organizations depend on a stable of average performers. Not everyone has the capacity to be a star. Ask yourself the following:

Can this person improve or is he doing his best? If the employee is underachieving, let him know how he can improve and what the rewards will be for doing so. If the employee is working up to capacity and the performance is adequate, perhaps the wisest course is to review him kindly without raising his expectations.

Are the person's expectations realistic? Sometimes,

subordinates have wildly unrealistic estimations of how well they're doing or their bright prospects for advancement. Sometimes they believe their title carries automatic authority or deference. If you believe someone has topped out, let him know while expressing gratitude for his contributions.

Watch out for personal pleading. Sometimes, employees have a genuine, temporary crisis in their lives, an illness in the family, for example, that merits special consideration. It should be given. But if blaming performance lapses on factors outside the job becomes a habit, the reviewer should find a gentle way to point this out.

## Recognizing Excellence

Commend the star employee in detail, so you can reinforce positive performance. In this situation, you're in a position to form a sort of partnership with the reviewee. Talk to her about the problems you're facing and invite her to participate in the solutions.

Make the rewards for achievement clear. Let the reviewee know she has your gratitude and full support. Often this involves providing counseling or resources for the person's future career path.

Think creatively about how you can provide the high achiever with new challenges. Make the review an opportunity to draw the person out on how she can contribute to the organization more effectively.

# A Final Thought

Don't start planning your reviews on Tuesday morning, an hour before they begin. Nothing reflects more on your own review than the performance you get out of your subordinates. Enter each interview with a tailored strategy to ensure that you get the best out of your team.

**Reprint C9905A**

# Performance Management That Drives Results

• • •

Loren Gary

Beginning in the late 1990s, Weyerhaeuser embarked upon a campaign to achieve market leadership in the paper and wood products industries through a series of acquisitions. After the last of these acquisitions, Willamette Industries, in 2002, executives at the Federal Way company conducted an assessment of the company's culture and realized they had a problem: they weren't doing a good enough job of holding leaders accountable for achieving superior competitive performance.

"The principles upon which the performance-management system was based were great," says John

Hooper, director of strategic workforce initiatives and change. "But we hadn't institutionalized them in managers' actions and behaviors."

Weyerhaeuser's leaders recognized that the organization was slow to address performance problems. "Eighty-two percent of the company's employees had received an above-average rating in the most recent evaluation," says Hooper. "There was also little correlation between individual performance ratings and compensation decisions. In short, we needed to walk the talk." So Weyerhaeuser set a task for itself: build a performance-management culture that would help it achieve top-quartile performance in each of its major lines of business.

> Only by putting A people in the A jobs can a company really move ahead of its competitors.

Like Weyerhaeuser, more and more companies are demanding that their performance-management systems drive demonstrable business results. And what they're discovering is that one-size-fits-all notions of performance won't get them where they want to go.

The most powerful systems for managing employees' efforts "respond to an organization's unique business and human capital context," write Colleen O'Neill and Lori Holsinger, of Mercer Human Resource Consulting, in a recent white paper. But even the most exquisitely tailored system can't run on autopilot—its success depends on executives' willingness to hold themselves and their subordinates accountable for delivering the desired results.

Experts say that performance-management excellence requires perspective, metrics, and a passion for execution. The best managers:

- Develop rigorous systems that create distinctions among three groups: the few who are making outstanding contributions, the great majority who are performing successfully, and the small number who aren't making the grade.

- Create measures to drive employee contributions.

- Foster a culture of accountability, in which supervisors aren't afraid to speak frankly when targets aren't being met, or to link decisions about financial incentives to actual performance.

## Addressing Relative Contributions

High-performing organizations clearly distinguish top performance from satisfactory and poor performance.

To determine the "right" method for doing this—more on the options later—senior leadership must first decide "what they value most about performance," says O'Neill.

For example, one of O'Neill's clients, a financial services firm, decided that, given its corporate culture, it was more important to identify and correct underperformance than it was to make subtle distinctions among the top performers. Weyerhaeuser has decided to do both: create gradations of difference among top performers and weed out underperformers.

## Get the Best People in the Most Important Jobs

Once you've identified the overarching goals of your performance-management system, create what Mark Huselid, professor of human resource strategy at Rutgers University's School of Management and Labor Relations, calls a "differentiated workforce strategy."

In a pharmaceutical company, he explains, the main drivers of extraordinary performance include the ability to tightly manage R&D cycle times, high-quality manufacturing processes, an excellent sales force, and a deep understanding of how to work with the FDA.

"These activities are the company's A jobs, its most strategically significant positions," says Huselid. For each A job, the company should "determine what the associated capabilities and workforce competencies, leadership behaviors, and key indicators of business success are." For the salesperson, one competency might be the ability to get face time with doctors; one success indicator might be the number of prescriptions written per hour spent with a physician.

"Only by putting A people in the A jobs can a company really move ahead of its competitors," says Huselid. "Spell out what extraordinary performance would look like for each of these A jobs, then make sure you've got your top performers in those jobs. B players, whose performance meets the basic expectations, also have a role in the company, but until they demonstrate that they can perform at A levels, they should not be in the most important positions."

## Know How to Handle Underperformers

"Do you really want C players in your company at all?" asks Huselid. "More and more businesses are culling their bottom ranks of employees with good results." His views about what to do with employees who aren't meeting basic expectations represent one end of the spectrum in a lively debate that currently rages in management circles. To some extent, the disagreement is a result of confusion over two different methods of differentiating performance, says Dick Grote, a performance-management consultant and author.

*Absolute comparison* procedures evaluate individuals in terms of their performance against predetermined goals and expectations, Grote explains. It's the approach that's commonly used in performance appraisals: "How

## Customizing to Fit Your Culture

Forestry products company Weyerhaeuser has tailored the forced distribution scheme it uses for performance management by opting for recommended rather than forced distribution guidelines. "At our company, leadership is not seen as a paint-by-numbers affair; rather, it's a matter of applying broad, overarching principles," says John Hooper. "Our senior managers basically said, 'We should be trustworthy enough to expect high performance ourselves and inspect performance ratings and compensation decisions ourselves to make sure that they're in line with the goals—we shouldn't have to rely on the performance-management system to make the distribution decisions for us.'"

The basic criteria for making these decisions are performance against agreed-upon stretch goals and the demonstration of certain key leadership behaviors. When necessary, additional criteria are used to help supervisors make finer distinctions. These criteria include comparing A players from different units to see if any meaningful distinctions in their performance can be made and looking to see whether some top performers have made a greater contribution to shareholders than similarly ranked employees.

This may not be the textbook approach to "transforming a 'nice' performance management culture into one characterized by 'tough love,' but it's working for us," Hooper continues. "At the end of the first year of using the new system, we saw significant differentiation among the performance ratings and also in the merit and bonus decisions."

well did Pat do against the objectives and competencies we discussed at the beginning of the year?" The problem with absolute comparisons is obvious: if the standards are set low enough, almost anyone can exceed expectations.

*Relative comparison* is different. Here individuals are evaluated in terms of how their performance compares with that of other people. It's this technique that makes many managers uncomfortable.

"*Forced ranking* and *forced distribution* are two examples of the use of relative comparisons," explains Grote. "A forced ranking system usually operates alongside but somewhat apart from the performance-appraisal process, using criteria that address both employees' performance and their potential." In a typical scheme, 20% of a company's workers are identified as A players, 70% as B players, and 10% as C players. Even if everyone is meeting basic expectations, some employees are still assigned to the bottom tier and, in some companies, terminated on the basis of that evaluation. This is the policy that raises the ire of many experts, who argue that it undermines trust in the corporate culture to terminate employees who are hitting their targets. But not all companies that use forced ranking automatically terminate the bottom-tier employees; some just notify employees of their rank without taking any additional action, says Grote.

A forced distribution system, on the other hand, focuses just on the annual appraisal process, not on assessments of employees' potential. "Perhaps 30% of Fortune 500 companies use this method to counteract the 'grade inflation' in performance ratings by ensuring that there's some differentiation," says Grote. For example, a company might decide that only 5% of its workers can be assigned a "distinguished" rating and no more than 20% can get a "superior" rating. The company might also require that 10% of all employees be assessed as "needs improvement" and that a minimum of 5% must be rated "unsatisfactory."

## Building Accountability

A robust performance-management system provides a structure that encourages executives to take responsibility for seeing to it that their reports meet their objectives and also that their reports hold their subordinates similarly accountable. It fosters accountability in two ways. First, it helps ensure that employees hew to the metrics that have been chosen to evaluate progress toward the stated goals.

At American Airlines, for example, a new online performance-management tool for management and support staff—some 10,000 employees in all—enables an employee to look up her entire chain of command quickly, so she can better coordinate the objectives she's setting for herself with the goals and metrics identified by the managers and organizational units above her. "Whenever an employee changes an objective," says Sarah Keller, manager of performance management, "the system sends an e-mail to the employee's supervisor. This creates an opportunity for the supervisor and employee to have a conversation about how well aligned the new objectives are, and whether the right measures have been chosen to assess its impact."

The second way a performance-management system builds accountability is by encouraging managers to be diligent and discerning in their appraisals. At Burlington Northern Santa Fe Railway, a "people leader" program brings supervisors at the same level together for two days each year.

Here they receive coaching from one another and outside experts about how to foster an ongoing dialogue with subordinates about performance, how to ensure that the company's strategic objectives cascade down to the individual level, and how to pick the right measures for evaluating performance.

When it's time for the annual performance review, a supervisor's manager reviews the supervisor's appraisal of an employee and that employee's self-evaluation before the actual meeting takes place. This allows the reviewing manager "to see if his impression of the employee squares with what the employee has accomplished," says Lachelle Ashworth, director of organizational effectiveness.

In other companies, managers two and three levels above the supervisor read these appraisals before the meeting is held.

"Although executives this high up don't have much day-to-day interaction with these employees, they still

## The Hidden Factors That Make or Break Performance Management

The best performance-management systems provide a framework for differentiating performance and for linking those judgments to appraisal ratings and compensation decisions.

But what makes individual managers willing to ask hard questions such as, "Why doesn't this unit's performance jibe with the ratings of the individuals in it?" What helps them make time available for the often uncomfortable work of coaching and monitoring an employee whose performance is subpar, or for the emotionally draining task of managing an employee who fails to improve out the door?

"No matter how much you fine-tune the processes, performance management will never be easy or simple," says consultant and author Dick Grote, "and even the best system can't replace the need for courage and perseverance." What helps managers tap into these emotional resources?

- **Clarity.** Managers who've already provided straight talk about what is required have a much easier time addressing problems that arise when those requirements aren't being met, says Grote.

have some subjective sense of where the real talent in the organization lies, some feeling for who is positioned to take the company into the future," says consultant Grote. "Being able to review the appraisals of employees two and three levels below them helps the senior leaders

- **"Senior executives** who make performance management a part of their persona," says Mercer Human Resource Consulting's Colleen O'Neill. Adds Grote: "You can't overestimate the value of having senior managers who show up at performance-management training sessions and who demonstrate genuine appreciation for the difficulties involved in supervising people by sharing stories of situations they've dealt with in their own careers."

- **Stretch goals, negotiated interdepartmentally.** Say a CIO is trying to set a stretch goal around reducing the cost of the computer assets used by the company's business units. "It's easy to set that goal in isolation, but if she has to do it in conversation with the leaders of the business units that will be affected by that goal, that's what really brings performance management to life," says Weyerhaeuser's John Hooper. "The CIO says she wants to reduce asset costs by X percentage, the business-unit heads describe the consequences that reduction will have for each of them—the conversation goes back and forth until agreement is reached. Leaders are more likely to own targets that have been collaboratively decided upon."

confirm or discount these subjective impressions. What's more, it allows them to see which supervisors are doing a good job of managing the talent they have."

Regular evaluations of the entire performance-appraisal process also help build accountability. At Sprint, employees provide comments on the process through an online survey sent at the end of the annual appraisal. Based in part on last year's employee feedback, Sprint has established a specific manager quality objective: in this year's evaluation process, employees will be able to assess the quality of their supervisors. Other companies hold rater-reliability sessions, in which supervisors share their ratings of subordinates before the appraisals are sent up the chain of command for review. By forcing supervisors from different groups to defend the ratings they've given their people, these sessions help to ensure a level playing field.

Of course, nothing makes managers pay attention to performance management faster than making the ability to do it well an essential criterion for promotion.

At Lucasfilm, managers' current performance assessments are based, in part, on how rigorously they have worked to develop their direct reports and how proactive they have been in identifying and addressing performance issues. These assessments become part of a larger evaluation of managers' potential for senior leadership.

Reprint U0409A

# Debriefing Robert Fritz

## Telling the Hard Truth About Poor Performance

• • •

**Lauren Keller Johnson**

An employee misses the deadline on an important project. An expensive marketing campaign delivers luke-warm results. A major division's revenues start slipping. No matter where you sit in your organization, you encounter performance that sharply differs from expectations. How you respond determines whether your organization learns from such moments and goes on to improve—or whether a pattern of repeated failure is established instead.

When confronted with subpar performance, many of us employ work-arounds rather than directly addressing the problem, write Bruce Bodaken and Robert Fritz in *The Managerial Moment of Truth: The Essential Step in Helping People Improve Performance.* Our reasons for this avoidance are understandable—and all too familiar. We feel we don't have time to correct ineffective work habits. We dread conflict and fear that painful conversations about substandard performance will destroy morale and drive employees away. And some of us work in organizations that discourage honest acknowledgment of mistakes.

But avoidance and work-arounds carry a high price, says Fritz. For one thing, he says, "when you shift work to your best performers, you put them at risk for burnout, and you underuse your workforce overall." For another, avoidance creates a vicious communication circle: You say nothing until your annoyance with a performance problem reaches unmanageable levels. Then you overreact—with an intensity that's out of proportion to the problem. Afterward, you're embarrassed by your reaction, so when the problem resurfaces (and it will), you once again say nothing.

But the most significant consequence of not acknowledging poor performance is that you deny yourself and your colleagues vital opportunities to identify what went wrong, determine which thought processes and decisions led to the problem, and develop plans for generating better outcomes next time. In other words, you miss the chance to activate a cycle of continuous learning.

To counter managers' reluctance to address problems head on, Fritz developed what he calls the *managerial moment of truth* (MMOT) process, composed of these four sequential steps: (1) acknowledge the truth; (2) analyze how things got to be this way; (3) develop an action plan; (4) create a feedback system.

Fritz and coauthor Bodaken betatested MMOT at Blue Shield of California (BSC) as part of a larger leadership initiative led by Bodaken, BSC's CEO. Bodaken and Fritz credit MMOT with fostering the better information flow and smarter decision making that have helped make BSC one of the fastest-growing health-care providers in California. The process, they report, works as well between colleagues as it does between managers and direct reports.

At the heart of the MMOT process is a thoughtful, deliberate use of questions. To illustrate what it looks like in action, we've used the example of you, the manager, talking with an employee about a missed deadline.

## Acknowledge the Truth

The first step of the MMOT process is removing the distortions created by biases, defensiveness, and previous experience so that both persons involved in the dialogue can agree on the plain facts of the situation.

You start off the conversation by stating the facts: "The project was due May 23, and now it's May 29."

Because many people find it painful to acknowledge a fact that suggests substandard performance, your employee may cite excuses ("I was swamped with other things") or blame others ("Sarah didn't get me the numbers on time").

> Not acknowledging poor performance can lead to a pattern of repeated failure.

To keep this part of the conversation focused on the facts, free of subtext, you may repeat: "The project was due May 23, and now it's May 29. Is that right?" Comments such as "You let me down" or "Missing deadlines is unprofessional" would be counterproductive because they only increase your employee's defensiveness. The aim of the MMOT process is to refocus the person from the subjective realm of feelings to the objective realm of facts.

## Analyze the Situation

Once you and your employee have agreed on the situation, you can work together to track the thoughts and decisions that led up to it. In essence, you're asking: "What happened first, and then what happened? What decisions did you make? Why did you make those decisions? What was the outcome of those decisions?"

Here is a dialogue adapted from Bodaken and Fritz's book that illustrates this step:

*You:* "What happened that the due date was missed?"

*Employee:* "The work took longer than I expected, and I got too busy with other things."

*You:* "When you were planning your work on this project, did you add the other things into the equation?"

*Employee:* "No."

*You:* "What does that suggest?"

*Employee:* "My planning was off; I should have looked at the whole picture."

*You:* "So it sounds like for future projects you need to make a more comprehensive assessment of your workload before agreeing on a deadline?"

*Employee:* "Yeah, that's what I should do."

Additional questions that can help track the sequence of events leading to the problem include "When you got the assignment, who was going to do what, and when?" "When did you realize the project was falling behind?" and "What did you do about the delay?"

Notice how these questions focus on the *employee's* decisions, assumptions, and thought processes—not others' possible contributions to the missed deadline. The person will come to understand that the relationship between the design of a process and its execution is critical to manage.

## Develop an Action Plan

This step builds on Step 2 to form a workable, practical plan to avoid similar problems in the future. The plan for improvement can be simple: "Take ongoing projects into account when calculating how much time a new project will take." Or it can be more complex with multiple components. But for the plan to catalyze improvement, it must be easily understandable and adaptable to the circumstances the employee is likely to face.

You should prompt your employee to suggest the action plan, providing ideas only if he has difficulty conceiving new approaches. Most important, ask the employee to document the agreed-upon plan—along with the truth you've identified and the events that led to the problem—in an e-mail or a memo. This demonstrates both sides' commitment to improvement and the document reveals how well the direct report understands these MMOT elements, enabling you to correct any misperceptions. The action plan should also include a statement about how its efficacy will be determined.

## Create a Feedback System

When your employee puts the action plan into practice, he may discover that the plan needs adjustment. For this reason, it's vital that the two of you establish a feedback

### A New Level of Honesty

Most organizations and the managers and employees within them value integrity and don't tolerate overt dishonesty. But when unspoken rules such as "Never argue with the boss" or "Don't admit mistakes" prevail, a subtle level of dishonesty becomes the norm. The managerial moment of truth (MMOT) approach upends this norm, say authors Bruce Bodaken and Robert Fritz in *The Managerial Moment of Truth,* because it uncovers the unspoken rules and assumptions that stand in the way of an honest assessment of the scope of a problem and how it came to occur.

"If you're a strong leader, you want people around you to tell you the hard truth," write the authors, and you "want to be able to tell the people around you the hard truth as well." The authors argue that true candor is obtained only when people commit to uncovering the truth together. "Groups that really tell each other the truth are the ones that ask each other questions," they write, and "seriously seek to understand opinions that are different from their own."

system that will enable you to identify where changes may be required. For instance, the employee could show you the project schedule as he is drafting it and review progress and address any difficulties with you regularly.

Talking about poor performance will never be easy. But when both participants in the discussion are well versed in the MMOT discipline and understand the objective of each step, they will find these discussions more comfortable.

Organizations that adopt the MMOT approach, Fritz says, not only will establish a cycle of continual improvement, but also will see workplace relationships improve and employees enjoying their jobs more. "People feel clean when they use this process," he says. "They know that there are no tricks—just honesty."

**Reprint U0607C**

# High-Performance Prison

• • •

*Jennifer McFarland*

A recent International Labour Organization study found that one in 10 workers suffers from stress, anxiety, depression, or burnout. But the blame cannot be pinned solely on downsizing or the pace of business. Employees—especially top performers—are often complicitous in their own exhaustion. Paradoxically, extraordinary achievement can give rise to fears that lead to burnout.

To understand burnout you have to take into account "the addictive, almost erotic, appeal that deep and obsessive involvement in a task can have," writes consultant Tom DeMarco in *Slack*. Highly motivated individuals are most susceptible, notes Southern Illinois University assistant professor Jo Ellen Moore. They "often have strong self-management skills and need little supervision; they can be counted on to know what needs to be done and do it." Not surprisingly, managers tend to overload these star employees, who "will work themselves to death to get it done." Adds DeMarco: "The high, the narcotic of gonzo overindulgence, and the associated fatigue all combine to reduce the individual's mental capacities." And if "they have any capacity left at all, they will use it to conceal the burnout, or at least to try to do so."

Psychologist Steven Berglas develops the addiction metaphor further in his book *Reclaiming the Fire*. Successful people cause their own demise, he argues, by believ-

## Are You a Candidate for Supernova Burnout?

Look at the following list of adjectives:

__Single-minded      __Unremitting
__Persevering        __Monomaniacal
__Self-reliant       __Zealous
__Assiduous          __Indefatigable

If you're over 40 and believe that at least four of these terms apply to you, then you're a "slam-dunk, guaranteed case of Supernova Burnout in the making," writes Steven Berglas in *Reclaiming the Fire*.

ing that everything will be all right—if only they can land the next project or clinch one more sale. But the expected psychological satisfaction almost never materializes. Success becomes a drug, and star performers constantly feel the need to score. "Once you attain a goal, you adapt to the high and the buzz wears off," Berglas explains. "Then the feeling of 'been there, done that' creeps in. Now what? You need higher and higher levels of the drug to get the desired psychological effect."

Underlying almost every symptom of what Berglas calls "Supernova Burnout" is "the feeling that the material, self-esteem, and interpersonal rewards accrued from success will be jeopardized by ongoing assessments of one's capabilities," he explains. "Consequently, in what should be a sublime afterglow following achievement, many careerists discover that they are blocked from initiating constructive changes by what psychologists call risk aversion." This fear of taking on new challenges manifests itself as *encore anxiety* ("What do I do next to top my last success?"), *entrepreneurial arson* (intentionally creating problems in order to relieve the boredom), and *self-handicapping behavior* (externalizing responsibility for potential failure by turning to drugs or alcohol).

Dealing with success-induced risk aversion is more a matter of "reconfiguring your gestalt" than of completely reinventing yourself, says Berglas. "Until you can see yourself as more than the sum of the component assets that can trap you on an identity-fostering-but-frustrating career path, you are vulnerable to all-or-nothing thinking about the consequences of introducing challenge, innovation, or change into your job."

To avoid becoming root-bound, repot your career periodically. If the economy makes it difficult to do that, make time for activities that invigorate you mentally. If your "self-esteem has multiple infusions of positive feedback and satisfaction," Berglas explains, "it is more stable, less threatened by the potential of failing at innovation and change."

---

### For Further Reading

*Reclaiming the Fire* by Dr. Steven Berglas (2001, Random House)

*Slack: Getting Past Burnout, Busywork, and the Myth of Total Efficiency* by Tom DeMarco (2001, Broadway Books)

**Reprint U0106D**

# Understanding the Power of Expectations

• • •

As many human resource experts have noted, a performance review is the ideal time to communicate what you expect from employees in the coming period. But conveying expectations effectively requires some care, as the articles in this section make clear.

In the pages that follow, you'll find potent techniques for leveraging the power of expectations to maximize your direct reports' performance. Ideas include inviting employees' input on the expectations you're proposing, linking expectations to each subordinate's unique and deepest interests, and focusing on desired future change rather than past performance.

# Great Expectations

## The Key to Great Results?

• • •

**Lauren Keller Johnson**

It all sounds so sensible: Expect the best from your employees, and they'll give you their best—a phenomenon that J. Sterling Livingston, founder of the Sterling Institute, discussed in his seminal 1969 *Harvard Business Review* article, "Pygmalion in Management." On the other hand, expect little from employees, and they'll give you meager performance in return—what INSEAD professors Jean-François Manzoni and Jean-Louis Barsoux have named the *set-up-to-fail syndrome*.

But the interplay between managerial expectations and employee performance is more complex than these commonsense maxims suggest. To be sure, expectations exert a powerful impact on an individual's performance.

Yet managers who believe that they've done their jobs merely by defining and declaring high expectations—without involving employees in the process—will likely get the same poor results that bosses with low expectations receive.

"The idea that setting high expectations gets you more out of employees makes sense at 35,000 feet," says Janelle Barlow, president of the consulting firm TMI US. "But you have to execute this principle on the ground." Experts and executives agree that successful fulfillment of individuals' performance expectations hinges on managers' ability to apply the following four practices.

## Involve Employees

Just because a manager wants a certain level of performance doesn't mean an employee can provide it. So managers need to find out what employees think of proposed expectations, notes Linda Finkle, a consultant with Incedo Group. Just as important, people are more committed to objectives they've helped to define and feel more confident that they can achieve them.

Bob Senatore, executive vice president of the staffing firm Comforce, invites employee participation in setting expectations by saying, "This is what I think we can achieve together. What do you think?" He and his reporting managers negotiate defined expectations, as do these managers and their reports. Then each manager-employee pair sets benchmarks for measuring progress, particularly when the employee is new in the role. Each pair also adapts expectations when changes in the business environment demand.

Ed Gubman, founding partner of Strategic Talent Solutions, urges managers to "think group, but see individuals. Big goals inspire people at the collective level, but you then need to work with each person based on their roles, strengths, and passions. You can't—and shouldn't— expect the same performance from everyone. You need to put people in situations where they can be successful."

## Focus on Achievability

No matter how actively employees participate in the expectation-definition process, they won't rise to the occasion unless they understand in concrete terms what's expected of them. Senatore says that Comforce managers express agreed-upon expectations with as much specificity as possible, including a target time frame for fulfilling each objective. They may frame expectations as, "We will sign a contract with this large account to provide them with five full-time and 10 part-time technical staff members through the first quarter of next year."

Other executives believe that too much detail can set the stage for a limited response; they maintain that clarity is still possible with less specificity. For instance, Ray Bedingfield, president of the executive search firm Woodmoor Group, tells recruiters who join his staff: "We expect you to be able to make six figures this year." He then leaves it up to them to decide what level of six figures to strive for.

Still, clarity of expectations isn't enough. Employees must see defined objectives as realistic and achievable. As Cary L. Cooper, professor of organizational psychology and health at England's Lancaster University Management School, says, "Expectations and performance are linked in a bell-shaped curve: High expectations can lead to improvement—until the expectations become unrealistically high. That causes overload, stress, and diminished performance. Yet many senior managers intuitively feel that they should constantly push their subordinates, setting ever-higher objectives and performance targets."

## Build Measures That Help Meet Goals

With the right expectations in place, managers should focus next on the measures that will help people to meet them, including feedback, training, and encouragement.

Sean McLaughlin, director of development and brand performance at Aramark Harrison Lodging, had this point in mind when he launched a new feedback program in 2003. He set up a system of e-mailed surveys to gather steady, specific feedback on service quality and

## The Power of Self-Efficacy

"Goals should be difficult," says James Smither, who teaches human resource management at La Salle University in Philadelphia, "but not so difficult that employees will see them as impossible and hence reject them."

Employees must believe they can achieve their goals if they try—a personal attribute that Smither calls *self-efficacy*. When self-efficacy is high, he says, people set more challenging goals. They also persevere when they encounter setbacks, and they respond to negative feedback with more effort rather than with defensiveness.

Smither says managers can boost employee self-efficacy by:

- Breaking up a large task and giving employees one piece of the task at a time, encouraging "small wins."
- Setting up work so that employees accomplish successively more complex and challenging tasks.
- Drawing employees' attention to colleagues who have surmounted similar challenges.
- Having an employee watch another skilled person model a desired behavior, whether it's performing a quantifiable task or exercising a harder-to-define interpersonal skill, such as conflict resolution.
- Expressing confidence in employees rather than focusing on criticism—or assuming that a person already feels confident about meeting defined expectations.

other criteria from hotel guests and meeting planners, the firm's two main customer groups.

The surveys, he says, provide "an enormous amount of actionable feedback that we can present to employees." If Aramark receives a response in which a guest or meeting planner has rated any performance criterion with a "1" or "2" (the lowest values on the five-point scale), the system sends an instant alert to the manager of the property in question. That manager must then communicate the situation to employees and devise a plan to address it.

McLaughlin says this approach "enables us to send two crucial messages: that we need to address alienated customers immediately and that we want to raise expectations as well as set them."

Feedback and training exert even more of an impact when managers add encouragement to the mix. As business coach Juliet Funt points out, "There's a huge chasm between a manager who says 'I want you to . . .' and one who says 'I know you can. . . .' Managers must constantly notice, affirm, and express thanks for high performance."

Nevertheless, "you need to adapt the form of praise you use," says consultant Ben Leichtling. "People want their praise in different forms—whether it's delivered orally in a public forum or personally in a handwritten letter or some other form. Through observation and trial and error, managers can find out which form each person prefers."

Likewise, people respond differently to criticism. "As employees work toward fulfilling expectations," Leichtling says, "keep letting them know that you expect the best they can give. If they have trouble fulfilling expectations, adjust your approach to each person depending on how they work best. Some people respond better to shock, disappointment, and criticism; others to help with building step-by-step successes."

## Tap into Employees' Deepest Motivations

"People are motivated to fulfill expectations based on their personal interests—not based on what others are telling them to do," says University of Houston business professor Curt Tueffert. "Managers must work with employees to discover what each person is most motivated by—whether it's competition, a chance to form close working relationships, or some other reward. When both participate in this process, each has a higher stake in the drive for top performance."

Management consultant Robert Cannon examines motivation from a different angle: "Most managers view the world from a problem perspective and use negative language. But no one is uplifted by the statement 'We've got a problem.'" Cannon helps his clients to use the appreciative inquiry method to frame expectations in positive terms. "Through appreciative inquiry, managers and employees can define together what's going well and which assets they've got to draw from. They envision possible desired future realities, then develop and implement doable solutions for realizing those visions. Instead of telling people how to do something, managers use appreciative inquiry to explain why it's important to do it. Leave the 'how' up to employees, and you get more ownership of those expectations and more buy-in."

**Reprint U0507C**

# Feedback in the Future Tense

• • •

Hal Plotkin

Last year, the staffing firm Kelly Services placed approximately 700,000 workers in new positions. The quality of the managerial feedback those workers received often determined their success or failure, says Steve Armstrong, the company's vice president of metro market operations. "It's absolutely at the top," he says. "Nothing good ever happens when the feedback is lacking."

This is gospel at a company that regularly solicits feedback from the corporations into which it places workers to determine how those workers did on the job.

But in many companies, feedback is something that is feared, avoided, or done halfheartedly at best. And that's a shame, because feedback is the key to unlocking the promise of continuous improvement. So how do you do it without alienating the very employees you want to help?

The answer is to begin by changing the conversation from one primarily about performance—the past—to one about change—the future. In other words, rather than blaming an employee for past mistakes, talk quite specifically about how that employee needs to improve. Give the employee a goal to work toward, not a legacy to overcome. Your ultimate goal "is to energize and excite people about the role you need them to play and the development they need to go through," observes Charles H. Bishop, Jr., in *Making Change Happen One Person at a Time*.

Managers and HR people need to assess employees' change capacity and not just their performance, says Bishop. When employees understand that they are expected to strive for continuous improvement, they are far more likely to take positive action as a result of feedback rather than resist it.

Not all employees embrace change; indeed, many are uncomfortable with it, and some actively resist it. It is essential that you, as their manager, communicate the high value your organization places on a willingness to change and improve.

When it is understood in that context, feedback becomes a welcome tool employees can use to achieve their own goals for advancement and recognition rather than an event to be dreaded. Formal, semiannual performance reviews provide an ideal vehicle with which to initiate or reinvigorate the feedback loop.

## Facilitate Feedback with a Six-Step Process

"If you do your job correctly, there will be sufficient ongoing communication so that all your employees know what is expected of them and how well or poorly they are doing," write Jack H. Grossman and J. Robert Parkinson in *Becoming a Successful Manager*. They recommend a six-step approach to facilitate feedback.

### Identify specific employee successes and failures.

Be specific. Don't tell an employee he is late too often. Instead, tell him the exact number of times he has been late during a defined period.

Be equally specific when offering praise, such as the amount of money or time a worker has saved the company. When talking with an employee, suggest Grossman and Parkinson, "focus on the actions rather than on your conclusions."

Indeed, one of the biggest mistakes a manager can make is to overlook the importance of giving feedback to valued workers. No one likes to feel unappreciated.

Roughly 25% of good employees who quit left due to lack of recognition, according to a 1998 survey by Robert Half International. Give too little feedback to your best workers and they may take their talents elsewhere.

Giving feedback to difficult employees requires an even greater degree of skill and sensitivity. In these situa-

> ## If you don't listen to employees, it's less likely they will listen to you.

tions, managers should keep in mind the distinction between factual and emotional feedback. Expressing anger or disappointment with the employee, either verbally or nonverbally, can be counterproductive.

In short, try to avoid letting your emotions get in the way. Instead, stick to discussing the specific behaviors at issue. And remember that communication is more than words: it's also body language, facial expressions, and tone of voice. The wrong moves in any of these areas can exacerbate problem behavior by turning feedback sessions into confrontations rather than constructive and productive exchanges. "If you try to deliver some factual feedback but your nonverbal signals indicate you are very angry, then the person is more likely to react with defensiveness or aggression," observes Robert Bacal in *Dealing with Difficult Employees.*

## Stop talking and start listening.

Ask employees to respond to your observations and pay careful attention to their words and body language; ask questions as necessary to make sure they've had a full opportunity to get their views across. If you don't listen to what an employee has to say, it's less likely he will listen to what you have to say.

## Discuss the implications of changing or not changing behavior.

If you are dealing with problem behavior, convey the probable outcomes in clear and unmistakable terms, such as the likelihood of being put on probation by a certain date, missing the next round of raises, or being demoted. Likewise, let performing employees know if they are on target to receive a bonus or other recognition. Specific information about consequences provides employees with benchmarks against which to assess and adjust their behavior.

A useful technique for dealing with particularly difficult employees is to take extra time to help them understand the organizational consequences of their behavior.

If an employee does not return customer phone calls promptly, for example, you might show her how her conduct affects customer satisfaction ratings. Make sure she understands the reasons she is being asked to do something. Armed with such information, employees are less likely to regard feedback as arbitrary or punitive.

## Link past accomplishments to needed changes.

Look for areas where the employee has been successful and point out how the traits that led to those successes can be applied to areas that need improvement. Don't just offer exhortations; build an employee's confidence by letting him know exactly why you think he will be able to handle whatever tasks are at issue. Explain how current workplace requirements are related to his previous accomplishments.

One excellent way to convey this type of information to workers who aren't getting it is by using group feedback to augment personal feedback. This can be accomplished by creating a nonconfrontational setting, such as organizing a division or workgroup meeting where a given subject, say improving customer satisfaction ratings, is discussed with no one being put on the spot. Encourage your best workers to participate in these sessions and get them to share their ideas and practices with underperformers. Draw out the discussions so that areas of potential improvement are highlighted and reinforced by the group. Then take the problem employee aside privately after the meeting to drive home any points that may be particularly relevant to her.

"The more sources of feedback available to a difficult person," writes Bacal, the more likely it is that he or she will "actually hear and act on the messages to make improvements."

## Agree on an action plan.

Ask the employee what steps he can take to address issues that have been identified. Solicit his suggestions. This is "a powerful tactic because people are more likely to follow through on their own ideas than on what they are told to do by someone else," note Grossman and Parkinson.

Make sure the specific ideas, timetables, and plans are realistic—and measurable, if possible—and then write those plans down and initial them along with the employee.

## Follow up.

Set a date and time to meet again for a formal review on progress related to the action plan. But don't wait for that date to stay engaged with the employee. Instead, use the development of the action plan as the starting point for the more regular, informal feedback sessions that distinguish a good manager. Let employees know when they are on plan and when they might be falling short.

The mystery about the timing or fairness of feedback is greatly reduced when the feedback is directly related to an agreed-upon action plan.

Keeping up this constant feedback loop in between regular sit-downs, suggest Grossman and Parkinson, also reduces the anxiety that often attends the more formal scheduled performance reviews.

## Remember to Express Appreciation

You should also be creative when it comes to providing ongoing positive feedback. Words of thanks can be the starting point, but there are many other ways to get messages of appreciation across, says Barbara A. Glanz in *Handle with Care: Motivating and Retaining Employees.*

Glanz suggests managers write letters and notes of commendation and put copies in the employee's personnel files. Or give workers a night out on the town, a surprise day off, tickets to a play or concert, or a gift certificate to their favorite store or restaurant.

If all this sounds like a lot of trouble, keep the stakes in mind. "People do not quit organizations," notes Glanz. "They quit bosses."

## For Further Reading

*The Complete Idiot's Guide to Dealing with Difficult Employees* by Robert Bacal (2000, Alpha Books)

*Making Change Happen One Person at a Time: Assessing Change Capacity Within Your Organization* by Charles H. Bishop, Jr. (2001, AMACOM)

*Handle with Care: Motivating and Retaining Employees* by Barbara A. Glanz (2002, McGraw-Hill)

*Becoming a Successful Manager* by Jack H. Grossman and J. Robert Parkinson (2002, Contemporary Books)

**Reprint C0211A**

# Selecting
# Performance
# Metrics

. . .

To determine whether your employees are delivering good performance, you need to define performance metrics—a major subject in its own right. And defining metrics is more complicated than many managers assume. The most effective metrics take into account not only an employee's job responsibilities and development goals but also the company's high-level objectives.

The articles in this section offer guidelines for selecting the right metrics against which to evaluate your subordinates' performance. In the pages that follow, you'll find advice for clarifying your organization's strategic goals, defining team- or unit-level metrics linked to those goals, and selecting performance metrics for each employee that further support high-level company goals.

# How to Think About Performance Measures Now

· · ·

Loren Gary

Now that the overall American economy is in recession, indicator lights on the managerial dashboards companies use to monitor performance are blinking red. Firms are taking a hard look at the tradeoffs between short-term cost-saving maneuvers and long-term growth plans. And those that are really up against the wall are scrutinizing their cash flow measures constantly.

"When the world changes, it's natural to ask whether you're measuring the right things," says David Larcker, Ernst & Young Professor of Accounting at the University of Pennsylvania's Wharton School. That is why key performance indicators (KPIs) are receiving a lot of attention right now. A KPI may focus on financial measurements such as days' cash on hand and operating income by unit or division, as well as the nonfinancial areas, such as mean-time response to service calls, cycle time, or percentage of sales from new products. But, as Larcker explains, the best set of KPIs should be viewed as a forward-looking system of measurements that help managers predict the company's economic performance and spot the need for changes in operations.

Is it time to reprioritize the measures you're tracking or adopt new ones altogether? In some instances, yes. But for most companies the problem is a disconnect between measurement and strategy. As Andrew Nelson, executive director of business strategy of Group Health Cooperative, acknowledges, "With our nonfinancial performance metrics, such as the customer service and work environment measures, we just don't have the depth of understanding of what drives our business." Before you start tweaking your KPIs, it's crucial to ask the strategic questions first: Is your overall strategy still sound? Do the measures you use really relate to it? And are you using the data you collect on your measures to reevaluate your strategic priorities? These questions may not help you avoid the tradeoffs that a recession forces on you, but at least they'll ensure that you make the tradeoffs knowingly.

## Linking Budgets, Measures, and Initiatives to Strategy

Of the 2,000 respondents to a survey conducted by consultant Lawrence S. Maisel and the American Institute of Certified Public Accountants, 80% said performance measurement systems were a way to achieve business results and create shareholder value. In practice, however, the respondents' performance measurement systems were focused rather narrowly on such traditional financial measures as cash flow, operating income, and sales revenue. That so many companies have taken up the performance measurement gospel is a development worth celebrating. But now that performance measurement has become all the rage, many firms are adopting the new terminology without understanding how their existing practices need to change. They don't really know what the key drivers of the nonfinancial areas of their business are, nor do they understand how these areas relate to each other or to the overall financial performance.

A KPI, in and of itself, doesn't tell you very much, says David P. Norton, president of the Balanced Scorecard Collaborative. Nor is the number of KPIs that you choose to monitor the most important consideration. The most crucial element, he says, is strategy: "You have to have a strategy first, and then you translate it into measures that you track."

The Balanced Scorecard concept, created by Norton and Robert Kaplan, Marvin Bower Professor of Leadership Development at Harvard Business School, is an outgrowth of the so-called value-based management techniques that first appeared in the late 1980s. It helps you highlight the cause-and-effect relationships among performance drivers and identify the links to strategic outcomes. But a Balanced Scorecard is not strategic planning, Norton insists. "It's a tool that forces you to articulate your strategy. You should be able to look at your scorecard and reverse engineer it to see what the underlying strategy is."

In addition to traditional financial measures, a Balanced Scorecard includes metrics that help your company answer three critical performance questions:

- How do customers see us? Metrics for this category include customer satisfaction, price relative to the competition, and market share.

- What must we excel at? That is, what internal business processes will ensure that we continually meet customers' expectations? Typical measures here have to do with cycle time, productivity, and quality.

- How can we continue to improve and create value? Metrics such as the percentage of sales from new products or the rate of improvement

in on-time delivery assess your firm's ability to
learn and innovate.

Many firms do their strategic planning backward, Norton continues. Their strategic plan lists initiatives and
uses internal business measures—time and cost metrics—
as milestones. But a strategic plan should not be about
managing initiatives. Your strategy should describe how
your firm intends to create and sustain value for its
shareholders. Typically, this overarching objective breaks
down into three component themes: *operational effectiveness* (improving the efficiency of core business processes),
*customer management* (understanding and leveraging customer relationships better), and *product innovation* (developing new products, markets, and relationships to sustain future growth). Operational effectiveness strategies
show results in the near term—12 to 24 months. Product
innovation strategies come to fruition over the long
term—two to three years for service companies, three to
five years for manufacturers, and as many as 10 years for
pharmaceutical firms. The payoff for customer management strategies is somewhere in between; segmentation
or service strategies, for example, often require two to
three years.

Only after these strategic themes have been determined should you identify measures for tracking your
progress. Next, establish stretch targets for the measures
you've chosen and then select initiatives that will help

you achieve the objectives. This helps you avoid the confusion of treating initiatives as ends rather than means. An initiative is a means of implementing a strategic objective, so the metrics should measure progress toward achieving the objective, not the initiative.

"Now that we're in a recession," says Norton, "the question is not, 'Should my KPIs change?' It's, 'Is my strategy still sound?' In general, the answer to that first question is no: strategy is based on a whole set of assumptions about customer value proposition, internal business processes, and learning and growth, in addition to financial expectations. If your strategy is still sound, then it should stay the same. But although the strategy doesn't change, the tactics do—the emphases within the strategy may need to change. I would implore executives not to overreact. I hate to see companies revert to unbalanced management in bad times."

## Balancing Productivity with the Need for Growth

Think of strategy as incorporating two contradictory perspectives: growth (a long-term perspective) and productivity (a short-term perspective). "You're always balancing the two," says Norton. "Although you don't eliminate managing for long-term shareholder value, right now you may need to be emphasizing the productivity

## The Evolution of Performance Measurement

Metrics such as "economic profit" and "residual income," which account for the costs associated with capital, help firms spot areas in which capital is being invested unprofitably. But these metrics, while value-based, are lagging indicators; they offer little help for "forward-looking investments, where future earnings and capital requirements are largely unknown—investments such as new product introductions or new market entry," write Michael C. Mankins and Eric Armour, partners in the strategy consulting firm Marakon Associates ("Back to the Future," *Journal of Business Strategy*). More holistic value-based management (VBM) techniques, introduced in the late 1980s, link strategy to finance, enabling companies to understand "the sources and drivers of shareholder value" within their businesses and "identify new and different strategies to create even more value."

The Balanced Scorecard, introduced in 1992, is just one example of how VBM has become more than a set of tools to use on high-priority issues. Companies' KPIs now include such nonfinancial measures as customer satisfaction, quality, and innovation, and the KPIs are linked to strategic planning and capital investment processes as well as to compensation and performance management schemes. Today, VBM is a holistic discipline sometimes referred to as "managing for value," connoting something every manager should be doing all the time.

issues more. But it's been so long since the last recession, many managers have forgotten—or never had to learn—how to deal with a below-average economy. If you're not managing to a strategy right now, you're short-changing your future."

Bill Cochrane, CFO of Saatchi & Saatchi, was at the ad agency during the recession of 1991. "Back then, it was basically slash and burn," he says. "We damaged a lot of client relationships in the process." This time around, there's a more surgical approach. When the growth rate of revenue by client started to slow in late 1999, one of the firm's bellwether measures—the percentage of revenue utilized by staff costs—started to climb. "That was our trigger," says Cochrane. "We started to furlough people, lay others off, and use more temps. But the Balanced Scorecard has helped us understand the importance of what we call permanently infatuated clients (PICs) to our business. We're cutting out everything that isn't client-focused right now. We're also evaluating activities that we've always done in-house to see if someone on the outside can do them faster or more cheaply for us. But client retention costs are minuscule in comparison to client acquisition costs. We're not going to do anything that jeopardizes our PICs—and so far, at least, we haven't lost any."

In the absence of a "do-not-touch" list of growth objectives, the outside pressure—from the board, investors, and Wall Street—to bring costs down becomes overwhelming, says Norton. The trick is to clearly communicate this balanced position, to focus on productivity-related issues without backing out of the long-term strategy. St. Mary's/Duluth Clinics Health System, a nonprofit health care network, started to get signals that the economy was changing right after it had developed its Balanced Scorecard in 1998. It responded by focusing on costs even more—this in an industry in which cost-consciousness is second only to cleanliness in its god-like virtue. But Dr. Peter Person, the CEO, has been careful to show the board of directors that these new cost-cutting measures won't hamper efforts to enter

> Use the data you collect to evaluate whether you're tracking the right measures and giving them the proper weight.

new market niches such as cardiology, orthopedics, ambulatory surgery, and imaging. "Especially now," Person says, "we need to be sure that we understand where our programs are profitable and where they're not. But we also need to execute our growth strategies as soon as possible."

"If you're up against it, you've got to focus on the short run," says Larcker. "Ultimately, it all comes down to the measures that can improve your cash position." For example: increase your sales, adjust your prices, generate more frequent inventory turns, minimize defects, and boost your productivity. If you aren't in such dire straits, a tiered approach that combines the short, medium, and long term—the operational effectiveness, customer management, and product innovation themes—makes the most sense.

DuPont Engineering Polymers, which makes plastic coating, has seen orders from its largest clients (in the automotive and electronics industries) drop off significantly. President Craig Naylor puts his blended approach this way: "The strength of the balance sheet is more important now, as is strengthening customer relationships. Yet I still believe in the net present value of the shareholder value approach. So we're looking at changing priorities based on a view of what will be permanently changed after this recession—that is, what won't get better when the economy picks up again."

## Adjusting Your Metrics

Always go back to your strategy before you even consider tweaking your KPIs. When you do that, you may conclude that some of the following advice makes sense for your company:

## Choose metrics further down the value chain.

Industrial firms that are more removed from the market-place—a fabric manufacturer, say, as opposed to a clothing retailer—can experience a bullwhip effect in downturns. When you reduce production by 10%, you cut orders to your supplier by 10%. Your supplier, in turn, reduces orders to its supplier by more than 10% because it now has excess inventory. This ripple effect continues up the value chain. The result, says Bruce Chew, senior group leader at the Monitor Group, is that "small changes in the marketplace lead to larger and larger changes the further up the chain you go. So instead of simply tracking your own order and sales figures, you may need to track end-customer sales and inventories of all the suppliers in your value chain" to get an accurate sense of which way the demand for your products may be going.

## Make sure you're using the right cost numbers.

"Full-cost numbers, based on accounting methods that track every dollar the company spends, may work well in an expanding economy," says Chew. But when the economy shrinks, they can sometimes give you a misleading sense of how a contemplated action will affect the economics. If you're thinking about cutting production by 10%, it's important to ask questions such as: Which of the activities that I normally do will go away in this scenario? To which vendors and suppliers will I not have to send the check that I normally have to write? And which assets will I be able to turn into cash? The answers will determine what your actual cost figures will be when you cut production by 10%. The lesson here: develop metrics for the specific decisions you're looking to make.

## Don't obsess over a single metric.

One of Chew's clients discovered it was at a 15% price disadvantage relative to its competitor—and in a falling market no less. The company calculated how many jobs it would need to eliminate in order to make up for the price differential. Focusing exclusively on head count, the company lost track of productivity: output declined as the size of the workforce shrank, and the 15% cost disadvantage never went away.

What's the right number of measures to track? Opinion varies fairly widely. "How many can a person keep in mind at one time?" asks Larcker. "I'd go with the magic number seven, plus or minus two." Kaplan and Norton, however, figure that a well-designed Balanced Scorecard should have 23 to 25 measures, and that no more than five should be financial. Suffice it to say that intuition still plays a role.

But don't get bogged down in the question. However many metrics you decide on, be a zealot about feeding the data you collect back into your analysis. Over time, you'll be able to see whether the measures you're tracking are in fact the right ones and whether you're giving them the proper weight. One firm Larcker studied, a corporation with thousands of retail outlets, became convinced that voluntary turnover among employees was the key driver of its share performance. Subsequent data analysis revealed a more specific metric—turnover among the managers of the retail stores—to be the real driver. Only after it got the measure right was the company able to launch initiatives—incentive and training programs for its store managers—that actually made a difference in the overall stock price.

"At the end of the day, it's not enough simply to say, 'Hey, our customer satisfaction measure improved 20%,'" says Larcker. "That's stopping a step short. For value-based management to be beneficial, you need to be able to see how your KPIs translate into bottom-line performance." Which is why "strategy is not a one-time event," says Norton. "You should always be reevaluating it."

**Reprint U0202A**

# Using
# Measurement to
# Boost Your Unit's
# Performance

• • •

If you're like most managers, you're drowning in statistics. Financial numbers. Operational data. Page after page of reports and tables piling up on your desk or hard drive. This information overload just gets worse as organizations install so-called enterprise resource planning (ERP) systems, which provide real-time data on an ever-greater number of variables. Mark Graham Brown, a performance-measurement consultant, reports working with a telecommunications company that expected its managers to review 100 to 200 pages of data a week. Other organizations pile on even more.

Data doesn't have to be the bane of your existence. In fact, it can be a tremendously powerful tool for managing your unit—if you know how to sort through it and how to use it to improve performance. Recent insights into the art and science of performance measurement suggest five key steps.

## Figure out the numbers that matter.

Any unit or functional department has to focus on only a few key measurements. More than a few, and pretty soon people get lost—or start finding ways to justify nearly any action on the grounds that it improves one or another metric. An HR unit might concentrate on average time required to fill a position, and on turnover rates. A product-development group might focus on development cost and time-to-market, both compared to plan. Any unit can come up with its critical indicators just by asking a few questions:

### What should our goals be in light of the company's objectives and needs?

Analyze your organization's situation and strategic objectives for this year. Is the company focusing on revenue growth? Increased market share? Cost reduction? Introduction of new products? There may be ways your department can contribute to these goals—and if so, the targets you set will be that much more meaningful for being tied in with a big-picture objective. This process is easiest if your company has already adopted a "balanced scorecard" or some similar system of explicit goal-setting. But even if it hasn't, managers in healthy organizations generally know the company's priorities and can choose key metrics accordingly.

## What will happen if we focus on a particular metric?

Brown calls this the "chicken efficiency" test. A fast-food chain gave lip service to many objectives, but what senior managers watched most rigorously was how much cooked chicken its restaurants had to throw away ("chicken efficiency"). What happened? As one restaurant operator explained, it was easy to hit your chicken-efficiency targets: just don't cook any chicken until somebody orders it. Customers might have to wait 20 minutes for their meal, and would probably never come back—but you'd sure make your numbers. Moral: a measurement may look good on paper, but you need to ask what behavior it will drive. You may be focusing on the wrong metric— or too much on only one of the right ones.

## Are we checking leading indicators as well as lagging ones?

Financial results (or performance-to-budget figures) are "hard" metrics, calibrated in dollars and nearly always meaningful. The problem is that they lag your performance. They tell you how you did yesterday or last month, but not how you're likely to do tomorrow or next year. For that you need "soft" or "perceptual" measures such as customer satisfaction and employee commitment, says William Schiemann, president of Metrus Group. "Perceptual measures are often leading indicators in the sense that they're highly predictive of financial performance." For your department, soft indicators might be measures such as employee turnover or surveys of internal-customer satisfaction. Track such measures today and you may find yourself worrying less about missing your budget tomorrow.

## Drill down to understand cause-and-effect connections.

Once you've chosen a few key metrics to track, the next challenge is to understand what the numbers are telling you. If defect rates have suddenly started to rise, is it because you're receiving lower-quality materials? Or because you recently hired several inexperienced employees? Most numbers worth watching are themselves the sum of many other numbers, and you need to "explode" the metric into its component parts so you can see what is driving the change.

Chris Howe, a consultant with Towers Perrin, reports working with a large utility company whose challenge was to reduce the cost of delivering a particular service.

## The Unbalanced Scorecard at Wainwright Industries

Walk into the "Mission Control" room at a Wainwright Industries plant, and you'll see five plaques on the wall, each one representing a set of performance measurements. "They're prioritized," explains plant manager Mike Simms—"not balanced but prioritized. If you do the first ones, the others will follow." The five, in rank order:

Safety, measured not just by accident-free days but by soft measures such as housekeeping improvements and number of employee suggestions relating to safety. (Wainwright's recordable accidents are down 85% since 1991.)

Employee involvement. One measure of EI is the number of suggestions for improvement received from each employee; the company shoots for 1.25 suggestions per employee per week. The other EI metric is employee satisfaction with "internal suppliers," which include managers as well as support departments such as MIS and purchasing. "People get the opportunity every three months to grade their managers," says Simms.

It turned out that labor cost was far and away the biggest driver of overall expense. So the team handling the problem mapped out every component of labor cost: wage rates, overtime, benefit costs, absenteeism, turnover, and so on. Breaking one "chunky" number—labor costs—into

**Customer satisfaction**, measured by regular report cards from customers assessing four key areas of the company's performance and by internal metrics such as on-time delivery.

**Quality**. "At Wainwright, quality is Job Four, not Job One," says Simms, an interesting statement in light of the fact that the company won a Baldrige quality award in 1994.

**Business performance**, including sales and net income. Both have been trending solidly upward for the last five years, despite the fact that Wainwright is in the fiercely competitive business of manufacturing metal stampings, machined parts, and assemblies.

Above each plaque is a flag—red or green—showing at a glance whether the company is hitting its goals in the area. Below the plaques are graphs and charts with the supporting data. Do people look at the information? Definitely, says Simms: "The room is used for training, so they're in there all the time." Also, he adds, managers sit down with each employee every three months to discuss the five areas. "We go over what the goal is, what the current number is, and what the individual can do to help the number get better."

its component parts enabled the team to pinpoint, monitor, and then attack key areas of potential cost reduction.

If your unit is relatively large, the key metrics may in fact be made up of a cascade of numbers, for which individual groups and teams within the unit are responsible.

A sales department, for example, might have aggregate goals for gross revenues, gross margin dollars, and selling expense; in this case, the overall goals would simply be the accumulation of goals for each product group or territorial team within the department. If the aggregate numbers don't turn out the way they're supposed to, it's easy to drill down to the component parts and find out where the problem is.

## Set real goals, not arbitrary ones.

It should go without saying: a metric without a target to compare it against is worthless. But a metric without a meaningful target isn't worth much, either. Too often, companies set goals simply by looking at last year's performance and tacking on 5% or 10% for improvement. Or else they set "stretch" goals that turn out to be ambitious objectives plucked out of thin air. (You can spot this kind of stretch goal easily, writes Brown in his book *Keeping Score,* "because they have nice round numbers like 10 or 100"—for example, a "tenfold improvement in product quality.") Brown advocates setting goals by analyzing your own past performance, your competitors' performance, the performance of "benchmark-level companies in similar businesses," your own capabilities (can you hit the goal given the resources available?), and input from employees and suppliers. "Competitors," incidentally, should be interpreted broadly. A functional department such as HR or IT can compare the cost of the services it provides with the cost of outsourcing those services, and establish goals based on that benchmark.

We'll discuss the element of employee involvement in more detail below. But it should also go without saying that the more people have a hand in setting a goal, the more they're likely to work hard to attain it. Goals imposed from above without rhyme or reason rarely motivate people. Goals imposed with rhyme and reason may or may not motivate people. Goals developed by a group that understands their importance are the most powerful motivators of all.

## Learn to forecast (and thereby to manage outcomes).

Your basic task as a manager is to see that your organization hits its objectives. The value of good metrics is that they allow you to monitor performance along the way. Still, even vigilant number-hawks often find themselves in reactive rather than proactive mode, responding to what happened yesterday rather than anticipating what may happen tomorrow. The most powerful technique for staying focused on the present and future is regular, disciplined forecasting. Weekly or monthly forecasting meetings typically begin with an assessment of progress toward the unit's goals. But then they turn to the upcoming week or month and ask where the unit is likely to be at the end of that time frame. This process allows people to talk about upcoming events and figure out how to cope with whatever needs to be coped with. Suppose, for example, you're responsible for a customer-service unit. You've focused on a few key metrics, such as average time required to handle a complaint and number of complaints that get bumped up to a supervisor or higher. You've set goals for improving performance. If all

## Tools for Tracking the Numbers

An effective performance-measurement system is easy to understand and communicate, and easy to use. Wainwright Industries tracks five sets of metrics, each with its own goals, and indicates on-track or subpar performance with green and red flags. Other companies have developed home-grown scoreboards or so-called executive dashboards. All these examples illustrate the importance of visual cues and graphics that enable people to see at a glance what's happening. At least one consulting company, Heath Corp., does a thriving business simply by helping clients set goals around key metrics, creating proprietary 18" × 24" graphic displays of each of these numbers, then leading the client's team through a monthly meeting analyzing progress toward the objectives.

The newest tool: software systems that track key data, provide managers (or managers and employees) easy access to the metrics they want to focus on, and allow drill-down capability at the click of a mouse but-you do is review the numbers, however, the response to suboptimal performance is likely to be, "We have to do better, folks" or "I'll see what I can do to get us some more resources." If you *preview* your performance, by contrast—forecast where you think the numbers will be at the end of this week or this month—you're forced to take action in advance so that they'll turn out right. And if plenty of people are involved in the preview, you can

ton. The software from Panorama Business Views, for example—a company that is one of the market leaders—provides numerical information in either a summary or "briefing book" format, with charts color-coded to indicate performance relative to plan (or any other benchmark that you set). Click on one of the figures and you can see where the number came from and where specific difficulties may lie.

Other suppliers of performance-measurement software include Gentia Software PLC, Show Business Intelligence, The Soft Bicycle Co., and Corvu Corp. Not every product is appropriate for every company—"they all have their strengths and weaknesses," says William Schiemann, president of Metrus Group—and the implementation process can be both costly and time-consuming. Still, dozens of companies around the world are finally using computers not just to hold reams of data but to organize it, communicate it, and make it useful to busy managers concerned with boosting their unit's performance.

brainstorm solutions whenever it seems that you're about to encounter a snag.

Forecasting isn't hard, even though everyone's first reaction will be, "How can we possibly know what the number will be?" Historical data provides a first approximation. Analysis of upcoming events helps, too. From then on, it's learning by doing: the more you forecast, the better you get. If the group challenges itself to forecast accurately within (say) a 5% range, it'll soon figure out how to do so.

## Don't go it alone.

Words such as "team" and "employee involvement" have already crept into this discussion, so you may have the idea that involving people in establishing their own goals and monitoring their own metrics is a good idea. It is. "Involve those closest to the action in defining the measures and setting the targets," advises Schiemann. Remember, however, that team scorecards or other front-line metrics are most meaningful when they're tied to larger strategic objectives. People have no difficulty getting behind a goal that makes sense in terms of the organization's business priorities. They have more trouble getting behind a goal that they don't understand.

One key to effective employee involvement is clear, simple communication of the numbers, over and over until people begin to understand them. A second key is regular meetings to review the numbers. "You have to have strategic review meetings where the issues on the scorecard are discussed in open forum," says Schiemann. "You come together to talk about the implications of the numbers, and about prioritizing issues." The meetings ensure that everybody is on the same page and knows what needs to be done.

Once you have your team monitoring key numbers and learning to hit the goals, you'll find that your unit's performance improves—at little or no extra cost. Then you can get rid of all those reports that are gathering dust on your desk.

--------

### For Further Reading

*Case Studies in Strategic Performance Measurement: A Council Report* edited by Ellen S. Hexter (1997, The Conference Board)

*Harvard Business Review on Measuring Corporate Performance* (1998, Harvard Business School Press)

*Keeping Score: Using the Right Metrics to Drive World-Class Performance* by Mark Graham Brown (1996, Quality Resources)

*Measurement in Practice,* quarterly newsletter (The American Productivity and Quality Center)

**Reprint U9810A**

# High-Performance Budgeting

. . .

Maybe you have just been through a cycle. Or maybe—if your company has a noncalendar fiscal year—it's looming ominously ahead. Whenever it hits, it's always the dreaded "B" word: budgeting. And it's nobody's favorite task. "In a retail environment the budget is out of date almost before it's completed," complains a manager for a large British retail chain, "but we still spend a lot of time and resources on it." Managers in other industries echo the gripe. Budgeting, so it seems, is nothing but an unproductive exercise that steals time from your real job.

Before you dive once more into a swamp of budgetary calculations and conundrums, however, consider an alternative view—namely, that the budget can be an immensely powerful instrument of forecasting, planning, and employee involvement. In fact, the budget can even help generate some excitement and enthusiasm around your unit. The trick to this transformation, as a handful of best-practice companies have discovered, is twofold. First you have to reengineer the budgeting *process*. Then you have to rethink how you use the budget *product*.

## The Limits of Budgeting

As background, it helps to understand what budgets can and cannot do. The traditional budget is a relic of an earlier industrial age—an age when top management's main jobs were managing capital and making sure the company recovered its fixed costs. Budgets reflected these objectives, just as they reflected that earlier era's top-down management style. Information flowed upward. Decisions flowed downward. The budgeting process allowed senior executives to allocate resources, while units' performance-to-budget allowed them to monitor the company's progress toward its financial objectives over the course of a year. Jeremy Hope, a consultant who has written about budgeting, calls budgets "the information superhighway—of hierarchies."

But while budgets may be a fine tool for managing capital in a slow-moving, hierarchical company, they have three critical flaws in today's economy.

- By themselves, budgets don't help companies focus on the performance drivers of today's businesses. Significant metrics such as innovation rates, service levels, quality, and knowledge sharing don't lend themselves to easy budgetary quantification.

- Budgets treat all employees the same—as costs. As any manager knows, employees' talent and involvement are more important in determining a unit's performance than the size of its payroll. On those measures, the budget is silent.

- The conventional up-and-down information flow of the budgeting process effectively compartmentalizes a company into small units. "You're judged on what happens inside your little piece of the action," notes Hope. "There's no incentive to look outside of that."

The problem is serious enough that a few companies are exploring radical surgery. Hope is one of the leaders of the "Beyond Budgeting" roundtable, a group of European corporations studying ways to dismantle their budgeting systems and replace them with something else, as yet undefined. Sponsored by the Consortium of Advanced Manufacturing–International (CAM-I), the roundtable includes companies such as Volvo and Schlumberger.

Meanwhile, other companies are finding ways to alleviate the pain of budgeting, not by eliminating the process but by reworking some of the assumptions behind it. This approach isn't as far-ranging as the roundtable's may turn out to be, and it doesn't solve all the problems of the budget. But it has one big advantage, which is that you can do most of it now, on your own, without waiting for senior management to decide that budgeting has suddenly become old hat.

The new approach to budgeting boils down to a six-point checklist:

## Begin with objectives rather than numbers.

Traditional budgeting begins with last year's figures: you take them as a baseline and add whatever you need (or think you can get away with). A better starting point is your unit's objectives, meaning what you want to see happen during the coming year. Laying out objectives not only provides a framework for discussion, it helps cut through some of the pointless back-and-forthing typically involved in budgeting. "I hear lots of people accuse senior management of asking stupid questions during the budgeting process," says Tom Pryor of ICMS, Inc., a training firm that teaches activity-based management. "But the questions are a sign that management has dated information. They will ask how many trips you have in next year's travel budget when what they should be asking is, 'What are you going to do with the resources we are giving you?' Clarifying goals can help them zero in on what's important."

## Check: Do your unit's objectives align with the company's?

Of course, your unit's goals need to fit with those set by upper management. For example, suppose you were a manager at CIVCO Medical Instruments. This year, says president Charles Klasson, the company wants to increase profit-before-tax by 18%. It proposes to reach that goal

---

## The Basics: Tips for Effective Budgeting

If you want to use budgeting as a planning-and-team-building tool, you need to develop a game plan. Even if you recently finished this year's budget, it's not too early to start thinking about next year. In fact, doing so can make it more likely that your budget requests will be approved. Here are a few points to keep in mind.

### Before the budget cycle starts:

- If you're a new manager, become familiar with your company's budgeting process.
- Spend time learning and understanding company priorities, as well as helping your team to understand them. Make sure any request for funds is in sync with the objectives set by senior management.
- Determine your unit's cost per output, however defined.
- Start gathering any information you will need, such as how your unit compares with other possible sources of the same product or service.

---

by focusing on the top seven OEMs in its industry, which account for 90% of the global market. If you were in sales at CIVCO, you wouldn't expect to get much money for developing new accounts. If you were in manufacturing, however, it's a good bet you could get funding to reduce defects to the 3.4-per-million level demanded by large customers such as Siemens.

If senior management hasn't clearly defined the company's objectives, it's up to you to set your own—and then ask whether they jibe with the big picture. "Define 'winning' for them," suggests Bill Fotsch, president of

> - Help team members begin learning about the budget. Ask for volunteers to research line items.
>
> ### During the budget-making cycle:
>
> - Start by drafting a preliminary budget that estimates your costs and outputs. If they're not within the parameters set by management, look for ways to make adjustments.
> - If you need to reduce costs, identify the activities that add value to the customer and those that don't. Analyze the cost of each, and begin by cutting non-value-added costs.
> - Show how your budget request will generate income for the company. In other words, your budget should be not so much a request for funds as a proposal showing how you will help the company realize its goals.

the consulting firm Great Game Coaching. "Tell them in quantitative terms, 'Here's what we see as winning for this year,' and ask them if that fits with the company's goals."

## Link the budget to performance drivers.

Budgets are financial numbers—dollars and cents. They don't measure those performance metrics mentioned above, such as quality and speed of operation. So you need to chart your achievements on those measures independently from the budget. The budget process should link dollars to drivers, however, by clarifying exactly what you expect to happen in each performance area if you spend what the budget calls for.

## Budget by walking around.

Old-style budgeting is the responsibility of the manager, period. He or she digs out the numbers, works and reworks the spreadsheet, then creates the justifications for the budget requests. A more effective approach is to turn budgeting into a team-building exercise, thereby creating what one manager calls "thumbprints of owner-ship" all over the budget. At Supertel Hospitality, a hotel franchiser with 63 properties, everyone partici-pates in creating yearly budgets. Even low-wage employ-ees may be assigned line items. For instance, housekeepers in many of the chain's hotels project how much linen and other supplies they'll need for the coming year, make a budget for these items, and assume responsibility for ordering them. Staffers work with management as well as with each other in figuring out how to keep costs down. According to CFO Troy Beatty, the process has contributed to lower turnover and higher profits.

### Keep it out of the file cabinet.

Once the budget is done, many managers file it away. A better idea: put it up on the wall (or on the intranet) and have team members use it to monitor their progress and achievements. At Seton Identification Products, a division of Brady Corporation, management reviews the financials every month with the budget owners, a group that includes a sizable number of people. This forces them to track and manage their progress. "I have to accurately forecast what I will spend and on what for each month," notes training and development manager Sheila Buckley. "Then at the end of the month I have to report on actual to budget."

### Explain the payoffs.

Some companies get employees to focus on budgetary targets by paying a bonus for hitting them. You may lack the authority to set such incentives—but that doesn't mean employees get no reward. "One incentive is the very fact that you're giving people responsibility and an opportunity to learn management skills," points out Buckley. Learning new skills helps people when it's time for a promotion. It also adds variety to an otherwise mundane job.

Once people do get involved, you're likely to find there's some excitement attached to making (or bettering) the budgetary numbers. That has been the experience of Bob Reczka, who manages the operator services division of TELUS Communications, a large telecommunications company. One of his division's goals has been to reduce the unit cost of operator-assisted calls, and to that end he is driving budget responsibility to front-line employees. Operators are learning to predict call volumes and to calculate the time and cost required for different types of calls. They're also being asked to find ways to reduce those costs. The response has been "unbelievable," according to Reczka; for example, people have already managed to shave more than 10% off the cost structure.

"Just engaging people in making decisions," says Reczka, "is rewarding in itself."

---

### For Further Reading

*Essentials of Business Budgeting* by Robert G. Finney (1995, American Management Association)

*Consultative Budgeting: How to Get the Funds You Need from Tight-Fisted Management* by Mack Hanan (1994, American Management Association)

*Transforming the Bottom Line: Managing Performance with the Real Numbers* by Tony Hope and Jeremy Hope (1996, Harvard Business School Press)

**Reprint U9901A**

# Of Metrics and Moonbeams

Five Keys to Evaluating the Performance
of Knowledge Workers

• • •

**Constantine von Hoffman**

In a manufacturing economy it's relatively simple to assess most workers' performance: just count the number of widgets produced and compare it against a benchmark or the worker's previous total. But if someone's job is answering calls at a help desk or contributing to the analysis of an industry or market, there are no simple metrics to calculate how well that person is doing.

Rudy Ruggle, director of Ernst & Young's Center for Business Knowledge, says that as the economy has changed from industrial to information-based, assessing how a worker performs has become not only more difficult, but more important as well. In an industrial economy, the most important things a company has are its manufacturing machinery and its factory output. Today, however, the most valuable part of a company's inventory is tied up in its workers' brains.

The need to know how a worker is performing isn't new, but "the intangible value involved has increased dramatically," explains Ruggle. "Now that the knowledge a company's workers have is so much more valuable, many people are realizing, 'I should be measuring this.'" Tom Davenport, a professor at the University of Texas at Austin's graduate business school, agrees, adding something mentioned by nearly everyone studying this subject: "There are many tools but none of them have been proven yet."

Nevertheless, useful advice does exist for managers looking to evaluate knowledge workers' performance. It largely consists of taking a systematic approach to the exploration of broad-gauged questions about the value of ideas, the definition of a customer, and the nature of your corporate culture.

## Put a Value on Ideas

How is an employee adding value to the company? Well, you say, she produces ideas—and ideas, as we all know, are the lifeblood of a corporation. But an idea is as ephemeral as a moonbeam. And there is a tendency to be distracted by sheer effort on an individual's part. "Is the number of new ideas per person important?" Ruggle asks. "If someone produces 100 new ideas and only ten of them are useful . . . and someone else produces only 20 ideas and ten are useful and one's a real winner—who's the most valuable?"

Everything in the business process must ultimately be aimed at the customer. Thus, to determine an idea's worth, ask whom it can be sold to. This is a simple question, but it has far-reaching implications.

To begin, think broadly about your definition of who a customer is. Internal customers are just as important as external ones: an idea that helps another person or department in the company work more effectively can contribute just as much value to the company as an idea that leads to new sales. Your accounting department and your customer-service desk clearly don't service the same people, but both groups are very important to the company's success.

Next—and this is particularly difficult—figure out who is responsible for specific ideas. Is someone originating concepts or just effectively applying ideas from other sources? Both types of worker are valuable, but they should be judged by different criteria. "How do you know when ideas are being used?" asks Ruggle. "People—for very innocent reasons—rarely give credit for the ideas they're using." To counteract this tendency, Ruggle advocates "making an explicit market in intellectual capital."

A call-in help desk provides an example. A company Ruggle worked with set up a system whereby when a call came in, if the person didn't know the answer, he or she could send a brief computer message to the other employees at the desk. Points were then assigned to those who provided answers to the question. This approach runs the risk of rewarding quantity over quality, admits Ruggle, but it does "set up an economics to getting a question answered."

Similarly, Ruggle's division of Ernst & Young has created an electronic repository of knowledge; people get credit for "deposits" they make to it. This system helps track who is thinking about what subjects. Ruggle hopes it will ultimately allow management to know who is "citing" whom when doing their work. This, in turn, can also help managers develop a knowledge map of the company: a detailed picture of who within the organization is considered to be truly expert on a given subject, or who is the person to see when you need to solve a particular problem.

## The Knowledge Tree Has Lots of Fruit— Not All of It the Low-Hanging Variety

When assessing a knowledge worker's performance, be careful not to focus solely on the obvious, immediate returns. Ideas that add value to the company come in two types, says Ruggle: those that contribute to know-how and those that contribute prestige. The second category can be as important as the first. It does you little good to be on the cutting edge in your field if no one knows it. "The purpose is not just to be smart but to look smart," Ruggle continues, pointing to the example of Xerox's Palo Alto Research Center (PARC), which in the '70s developed the now-ubiquitous GUI (graphical user interface) for computers. Although it was Apple and Microsoft that wound up profiting directly from the GUI, the development was still a huge boost to the prestige of Xerox; to this day, PARC retains its position as a premier research facility. By increasing your company's desirability to customers and employees alike, prestige eventually shows up on your bottom line.

## Whom You Ask Is Just As Important As What You Ask

Your overarching goal is to find and assess the originators of ideas that add value to the corporation, but don't give the information-gathering process short shrift. Don't just seek out the managers you're chummy with when asking who adds value, advise Ruggle and Davenport. Cast your net widely, even soliciting the observations of (gulp!) people who aren't managers.

Creating such a dialogue not only gets people thinking about a crucial subject, it also helps managers find out how workers perceive their role. Two fundamental tenets of management are that workers need to know what is expected of them and that managers need to know what those under them think the expectations are. "You need to ask people what *they* think their value is," explains Davenport, rather than assume you know the answer. After all, how employees assess the value of the knowledge being produced often depends on what they perceive their jobs to entail, beyond the formal description. "If you don't know what they think their job and contributions are, how can you assess what they are contributing to the company?" asks Ruggle.

## Tailor the Metric to the Specific Job

William Schick, who works for a computer consulting firm, has been on the receiving end of various assessment methods for knowledge workers. "It used to be that they were just counting the dollar value of the revenue you sold," says Schick, who has a dual role as consultant and sales facilitator. "Now it's how much did you sell *and* how many pages of systems documentation did you write."

Although the reason for this change was to take the subjectivity out of the job performance review, Schick believes it hasn't worked: "It still comes back to how good is your relationship with your manager. There are some quantities you can never measure." What you need to do an assessment, he adds, are "fairly crude measures of what the company needs plus what do others think of the worker." Thus, Schick is a big believer in 360° evaluations because they involve feedback from all the people—manager, peers, direct and indirect reports, as well as customers—who deal with an employee.

Even though 360° reviews can provide a more comprehensive picture of how an employee is functioning, there's no getting around the lack of a single metric that can be applied to all knowledge workers. Where you might judge consultants on the number and depth of relationships they have developed within an industry, you might want analysts to stay as objective as possible and not develop relationships that might color their opinions. With stock brokers, it might be totally inappropriate to judge them on anything but a bottom-line basis. So any metric you develop will have to be tailored to both the industry and the particular job. The difficulty in doing this, Schick believes, explains why many companies are now going to assessments and rewards determined by members of the team, relying on peer pressure to ensure that workers do their best.

## Know Your Corporate Culture

To evaluate workers adequately, you have to understand the corporate culture that serves as the backdrop for individual performance. This is especially true for knowledge workers, who are often motivated more by the opportunity for continual learning than by money.

How does your company behave? What does it consider important? What kind of person does your corporate culture encourage and/or discourage? "Questions about organizational culture are becoming more prevalent," notes Steve Hunt, senior consultant at SHL, an international human-resource consulting firm. "There's no ideal corporate culture, but you need to know what your strengths and weaknesses are." For example, does your company reward efficiency but not innovation and development?

Schick says that although his firm needs people who stay abreast of developments in the field, it doesn't provide them the opportunity to do so, or reward those who do. The result, increased worker dissatisfaction, doesn't surprise Professor Davenport. He cites a study of software developers that found—contrary to what most managers assume—that the developers were motivated by what they learn, not what they earn. In a tight employment market, in which identifying and holding on to your valued employees are keys to staying in business, this kind of information is pure gold.

Knowledge workers like to be on the cutting edge of their specialty, Davenport says. If your corporation doesn't encourage this, it is foolish to punish those who don't keep up. And you shouldn't be surprised when those who want to know more leave.

When thinking about your corporate culture, consider the values you want it to reflect and reward. And when thinking about rewards, don't think just in terms of money. "We have to make it clear that the most valuable thing is the ability to learn," Davenport concludes. Despite the gossamer-and-starlight quality of many attempts to evaluate knowledge workers, recognizing and rewarding the ability to learn in ways that serve strategic purposes should be the cornerstone of any system you put in place.

---

### For Further Reading

*Intellectual Capital: The New Wealth of Organizations* by Thomas A. Stewart (1997, Currency/Doubleday)

*Working Knowledge: How Organizations Manage What They Know* by Thomas H. Davenport and Laurence Prusak (1997, Harvard Business School Press)

**Reprint U9802A**

# Leveraging 360-Degree Feedback

• • •

Have you decided to introduce 360-degree feedback to evaluate your employees' performance? Or have you been using this methodology and want to improve its effectiveness? In either case, you may want ideas for getting the most from this controversial tool—which entails gathering feedback on an employee's performance from his or her manager as well as peers, subordinates, and (in some cases) even customers and suppliers.

The articles in this section provide ideas for maximizing the value of 360s. Suggestions include clarifying its purpose (for example, to create a more open culture), augmenting quantitative ratings from respondents with qualitative comments on the employee who's being evaluated, and introducing 360s initially as a professional development tool rather than a device for making compensation and promotion decisions.

# Should You Use 360° Feedback for Performance Reviews?

• • •

**Edward Prewitt**

By now, you're probably familiar with the basic idea of 360° feedback: gathering input on employees' performance not only from managers and supervisors but also from peers and direct reports. Most Fortune 1000 companies use or have used the method—also known as multi-source, multirater, or full-circle feedback—somewhere within their organizations, maybe because it seems to suit the current era of teams and flat organizations so well.

But most companies have limited 360 to developmental exercises, such as team building and management preparation. Now a few are venturing into the controversial realm of using it for performance review, with the multiple appraisals tied to critical decisions such as salaries and promotions.

In the Multisource Feedback Forum, for example—a six-year-old informal consortium of large organizations in various industries—"the big debate we're hearing right now is whether to use multisource feedback for performance evaluation," says Carol Timmreck, an internal consultant for Shell Oil's Human Resources Firm, who cofounded the forum. So far, the group's answer to that question is mixed. A recent survey found that of 15 participants who reported using multisource feedback for performance review in 1994, seven had ceased to do so by 1997. Yet other firms in the consortium began using it for appraisal during the same period, while still others said they intended to do so soon.

Here's the thinking behind extending 360 to performance reviews. Because most employees today work with a wide range of other people, no single manager can accurately assess their contributions. "Managers have so little opportunity to observe people's work because so much of it takes place outside," notes Kathy Almaney, senior vice president for human resources in the Corporate and Institutional Services unit of the Northern

Trust Company, a trust and asset management firm. "So in the [traditional] performance evaluation, they had little to talk about. We were interested in getting a broader view with 360." Getting that broad view of employees' behavior is a waste of money and effort, however, if it doesn't lead to improved outcomes. So companies want to link individual behavior to company goals. In offices that put a premium on, say, teamwork or responsiveness to customers, 360° feedback allows team members to comment directly on an employee's success in fulfilling those objectives.

But some think using 360 for performance reviews is risky—in particular, that it's dangerously naive about the human propensity to create hierarchies, protect status, and take revenge. "[Opponents] believe that using 360 for appraisal violates the condition of psychological safety that is necessary when giving a person dissonant information about the self," writes Maxine Dalton, a research scientist at the Center for Creative Leadership (CCL), in an overview of 360 uses. In other words, those who rate a boss or a peer may feel highly uncomfortable about giving a frank evaluation. Walter Tornow, the lead author of a recent CCL book on 360° feedback, says, "It takes a lot of trust in an organization and a lot of readiness before you can go from using 360 strictly for development to using it for decision making and performance appraisal. Many companies are not ready."

Is yours? Here's what practitioners and consultants say about making 360 work in performance reviews:

## Start with Development

If your organization hasn't previously used 360° feedback, it's best to introduce it purely as an internal tool for individual development and growth. "360 is a very basic change; it's very frightening to a lot of people to think that they're being rated by their subordinates as well as other coworkers," says Diane Irvin, vice president of Listen Inc., a 10-year-old consulting firm that specializes in setting up 360 programs. "If it's introduced as a performance development tool, then it serves to partner the individual with the organization."

Companies typically have a program in place for at least a year—often several—before attempting to link it to performance reviews. "Our recommendation is to spend a year getting people used to it," says Timmreck. A major manufacturer studied by Maxine Dalton did two years' worth of 360° feedback without seeing any change in the organization. In the third year, the program "took root" and began to be seen as an integral part of the company's functioning.

## Experiment with One Department

Tornow suggests focusing first on a single department or division that seems most ready for 360. In the two years since Northern Trust began its first program, the method has spread to other units; it's now used by 1,300 of 7,500 employees.

## Tie It to a Clear Company Goal

No program as unorthodox as 360 should be taken lightly; it must be introduced for a significant business reason that is plain to everyone. "The first step in creating a 360 program is to be very clear about why a company wants it: to change the culture, for instance, or to enhance the performance management system," Tornow says. "Hopefully the reason it's implemented is not because someone heard about it or read about it and said, 'Let me have one of those.'"

## Train Everyone Involved

Listen Inc. conducts training sessions for everyone who might potentially fill out a feedback questionnaire. The firm addresses issues such as confidentiality, data quality, who sees the composite reports, and how they are used. "Trust is one of the keys to getting accurate data," says research director Rim Yurkus. David Bracken, a consulting psychologist based in Atlanta and another cofounder of the Multisource Feedback Forum, notes

167

# Using 360 for Performance Reviews? Tips for Success

Based on their research at the Multisource Feedback Forum, Carol Timmreck and David Bracken have created 11 guidelines for instituting and sustaining 360° feedback in performance reviews:

- Make sure the program's sponsors within the organization have clear expectations for the process
- Make sure the sponsors understand the implications of their process-design decisions
- Use pilot groups
- Train both raters (those who fill out reports) and ratees (those who are rated)
- Train the managers who will use the data for decisions
- Communicate progress frequently and thoroughly
- Hold raters accountable for their input
- Involve raters in feedback and action planning
- Hold ratees accountable for feedback and action planning
- Implement follow-up processes to ensure compliance
- Provide adequate resources for coaching, counseling, and skill development

Outside consultants may be useful at several points in this process; they can reassure both raters and ratees that the feedback will be used objectively and appropriately.

that "one way we encourage people to give honest feedback is through training."

In Almaney's experience, managers are the key to success. "It all depends on the managers how well this is
used. Do they view this as a constructive process or as
a punitive process? We found it wasn't enough for the
manager to just get the report and then sit down with
the person. We had some training on how you use this.
It's human nature to immediately rush to the negative
on a report, so we trained managers to focus on the positive, because that's where the real leverage in improving
performance comes from."

## Follow Up

The feedback obtained in a 360 review shouldn't end
with a report, but instead should go into an action plan
for improvement. Without a formal plan agreed on by
supervisors, an employee "could totally misinterpret the
results and come up with a wrong [personal] action
plan," Timmreck says. The action plan should be tied
to results as well as to organizational rewards and pun-
ishments, Bracken argues. "The focus is on accountability. Are ratees being held accountable for doing something with the results of the feedback? If they're not,
they can simply ignore [the findings] and go on their
merry way."

# Don't Try It in an Atmosphere of Distrust and Fear

"If you have a culture that tends to be retaliatory and punitive, this might not work well," warns Almaney. Irvin says Listen Inc. won't knowingly work with companies that are downsizing. "In that kind of atmosphere, where everyone's afraid for their jobs, it can so poison people against 360 they'll never want to use it again."

In fact, for 360° feedback to be effective, it's helpful for a company to have in place a culture of learning and individual growth, says Jamie Higgins, a senior consultant who specializes in feedback programs at the Monitor Company. "If a manager is going to receive 360 feedback, but during the previous year, (1) hasn't asked for feedback, (2) hasn't acted on feedback they've received thus far or hasn't seemed to take it seriously, or (3) people feel some kind of retribution is going to happen, then by the time we get to the feedback program, there may be an atmosphere of mistrust and fear." Unless there's a more positive climate, she adds, "360° feedback can be of limited value."

---

### For Further Reading

"Using 360-Degree Feedback Successfully" by Maxine A. Dalton (*Leadership in Action*, winter 1998)

*Maximizing the Value of 360-Degree Feedback* by Walter W. Tornow, Manuel London, et al. (1998, Jossey-Bass Inc.)

"Multisource Feedback: A Study of Its Use in Decision Making" by Carol W. Timmreck and David W. Bracken (*Employment Relations Today,* spring 1997)

"Don't Tie 360 Feedback to Pay" by Dennis E. Coates (*Training* Magazine, September 1998)

"Working Smarter: Reforming Employee Development," a video toolkit based on the writing and research of HBS professor David A. Garvin (1997, Harvard Business School Publishing)

*360-Degree Feedback* by Mark R. Edwards and Ann J. Ewen (1996, American Management Association)

**Reprint U9902C**

# The Ratings Game

## Retooling 360s for Better Performance

• • •

**Lauren Keller Johnson**

After earning its stripes in professional development, the 360-degree feedback tool—which combines input from supervisors, peers, and direct reports to provide a broad perspective on an employee's strengths and developmental needs—has insinuated itself into the performance appraisal processes at an increasing number of companies. But as some firms are discovering, the colleague-based feedback that has made 360s such a favored tool in development can be its Achilles' heel in performance reviews: most human beings possess a deep ambivalence about wielding power over a peer's livelihood.

The majority of managers filling out 360-degree feedback reports hesitate to criticize any aspect of their peer's performance, particularly when raises and promotions may be on the line. Some also worry that negative feedback would strain their relationship with colleagues if it ever came out who had provided which ratings. And then there is the quid-pro-quo dilemma. As former General Electric CEO Jack Welch notes in *Jack: Straight from the Gut*: "Like anything driven by peer input, the system is capable of being 'gamed' over the long haul. People [at GE] began saying nice things about one another so they all would come out with good ratings." On the flip side, vindictive sorts might take advantage of an opportunity to besmirch a colleague's professional reputation. In the end, this leaves a great many managers dreading their involvement in 360s, whether as a subject or as a contributor.

So is the use of the 360-degree feedback tool for performance appraisals a mistake? Some experts say yes: it should be left to its original purpose. But others disagree, pointing to new ideas on reshaping the tool so that it not only encourages direct and honest feedback in annual reviews but also fits the particular needs and priorities of a broad range of organizations.

## Development to Appraisal

It's easy to see why firms are attracted to using the 360-degree approach for performance appraisals. After all, it promises a much more comprehensive picture of a manager's performance than the traditional boss-only review can offer. As Ginka Toegel and Jay A. Conger point out in "360-Degree Assessment: Time for Reinvention" (*Academy of Management Learning & Education*, September 2003), firms that use it for both development *and* appraisal get more bang for every buck they've invested in it. In addition, the authors point out, "flatter organizational structures [have] loosened the link between reviews and promotions," eroding the meaningfulness of traditional performance appraisal approaches and causing "growing dissatisfaction with the review process." What better way to address this dissatisfaction than to use a proven professional-development tool that's already near at hand?

But as companies have chalked up firsthand experience with using 360 for performance evaluation, they've run into problems. For one thing, obtaining distorted feedback wastes the time and money invested in adapting and using the tool. Equally troubling, recipients may well view the feedback process as punitive—and studies have shown that punishment is far less effective than reward and encouragement in enabling change. As Toegel and Conger acknowledge, "opponents of the migration toward appraisal argue that the goal of 360-degree assessment should be broader than simply assessing performance: it should foster continuous learning and personal development. . . . Using the 360-degree data for performance appraisal makes the developmental process potential 'punitive' and one that is 'forcing' instead of 'enabling' change."

To address such concerns, Toegel and Conger advocate creating two separate versions of the 360: one for professional development and the other for performance appraisal. The development version should rely more heavily on qualitative feedback, the appraisal version on quantitative responses. In the appraisal version, metrics would relate to measurable performance outcomes such as quality, quantity, and cost. Moreover, they say, reviewers should indicate the extent to which constraints such as high turnover and loss of funding have influenced the individual's performance. The recipient and his supervisor would then discuss how constraints might be eliminated in the future.

Others say organizations using 360s for performance appraisals are making a bad mistake. "Tools like the 360 get a buzz, and then companies faddishly adopt them without appraising what they want from them, or their effects," says workplace psychologist Ken Christian. "Then they make matters worse when no one asks, 'What's our purpose in using a personal development tool for performance appraisal?' With the 360, you can't keep feedback anonymous, so it's a sham exercise. Any potential developmental benefits of the tool are lost."

Even so, executives from companies across a broad range of industries continue to use 360s. And some are creatively addressing the problems inherent in using the tool as an appraisal device—and generating promising results. To get the most from 360s in performance appraisal, attend to the following key principles:

## Base feedback on crystal-clear criteria.

Some companies have discovered that the numerical rating scales commonly used to score recipients' performance generate meaningless information. This is especially true when the scales are used to rate hard-to-quantify managerial qualities such as "communication ability" or "integrity." Yet according to Bob Speroff, director of human resources–operations support at FedEx Express, there *is* a way to develop quantifiable criteria.

Speroff's organization currently gathers performance feedback from managers' supervisors, direct reports, and peers through separate mechanisms that the company has developed. Supervisor feedback comes from the traditional annual performance review process. Direct reports' feedback is derived from surveys in which employees comment on their manager's leadership abilities. And peer feedback comes from surveys of "internal customers," as managerial peers at FedEx Express are known. All the data is compiled and then tied to compensation.

Not surprisingly, the peer portion of the feedback has posed the thorniest problems because peers do not always provide the most candid commentary on one another. Speroff says scores average 3.6 on a 4-point scale, suggesting near-perfect performance. But business *results*—in particular, earnings per share—aren't always that stellar for each divisional group. Clearly, a disconnect exists between the performance feedback and actual performance.

To address it, Speroff's group plans to change the peer-feedback component of the traditional 360. Specifically, rather than rating colleagues on hard-to-quantify criteria, peer managers will evaluate one another according to how well they meet measurable internal customer/supplier service agreements the parties have forged. For example, Speroff explains that "if I promise an internal customer—a VP of a division—that my group will hire 2,000 new employees for her division at a recruiting cost of $4,000 each, and that the turnover rate will be less than 20%, it'll be pretty easy to see if I've fulfilled those commitments."

With Speroff's new approach, there's only one criterion for excellent performance: Did a manager meet his commitments to the internal customer? This simplified approach enables the organization to avoid the political maneuvering and the squeamishness about giving negative feedback that are inherent in the current rating system.

### Customize and stretch the tool.

FedEx's approach illustrates another key principle to more effective use of the 360: customization of the tool.

In FedEx's case, the company's plan does not impose one-size-fits-all performance standards on managers. Rather, internal customer/supplier pairs define the standards—in terms of service agreements—against which performance gets measured. Peers evaluate one another's performance based on objectives *they've* identified as most important to their ability to excel within the company.

Francie Dalton, president of Dalton Alliances, a communications and behavioral sciences consultancy, agrees that having 360-degree feedback recipients participate in defining performance criteria offers major advantages. "Recipients perceive the results of the review as more valid," she says. "They also tend to feel more committed to acting on the results—a necessity for spurring change."

Some firms and individuals are finding other creative ways to customize use of the 360. As Joann S. Lublin notes in the *Wall Street Journal*, Pfizer CEO Henry McKinnell posted "25 senior executives' evaluation of his performance . . . on the drug company's internal Web site early last year." McKinnell's goal? To enable every worker to "learn about his strengths and weaknesses."

William Arruda, founder of the branding consulting firm Reach, encourages his clients to include feedback from people *outside* their organization—such as customers, business partners, suppliers, and other external constituencies. "Business today," Arruda explains, "is more about your success outside the organization than inside. Getting feedback from external constituencies reminds you that outsiders' perceptions are important.

You begin behaving more as a team player with people you wouldn't normally make yourself visible to."

Dalton advises client firms to combine individual 360-degree feedback results into group scores. "This approach protects anonymity yet still sheds light on how a group or department is perceived collectively." For example, do members of a particular team "perceive their own group as being empowering? As backbiting? By getting a sense of their group's overarching characteristics, individual team members can begin gaining insights into whether they're pulling the team up or dragging it down."

## Don't skimp on qualitative feedback.

Laurent Charpentier, head of Ford's customer service division–France, says managers have responded well to an increase in the qualitative-to-quantitative feedback ratio in the company's 360-degree surveys. Managers had viewed the quantitative-only metrics used in the previous version of the tool as "too impersonal," he says. Once the qualitative component was added, managers found the feedback "much more effective."

Toegel and Conger agree that quantitative feedback alone can't capture the subtleties and nuances that written comments can. Yet they advise against providing extensive qualitative feedback in 360 surveys used for performance appraisal. Rather, they recommend a heavy emphasis on written comments only when the tool is used for professional development. In this case, they explain, reviewers should provide qualitative feedback to explain and justify every numerical evaluation on the survey. The authors also suggest putting questions requiring the most extensive qualitative responses early in the survey form, so reviewers can fill them out before "respondent fatigue" sets in.

## Clarify the tool's purpose and structure.

Many managers have found that communicating the 360's purpose and applying it according to a clear, predictable structure can increase its effectiveness. In Charpentier's division, for example, everyone who will receive 360-degree feedback first gets an explanation of the evaluation's purpose: to help her define areas for improvement—not to determine compensation. At year's end, managers receive an annual 360-degree appraisal from which they set their own objectives for the coming 12 months. Then, the following year, they receive coaching on areas needing improvement at midyear, the end of the third quarter, and at year's end.

Duff Young, CEO of Rehrig International, a shopping cart manufacturer, agrees that using the 360 to a clearly defined end is essential. For instance, he has seen executives who are squeamish about delivering bad news use the tool to amass negative feedback and then "dump" it on the hapless manager. Young now encourages executives to address performance concerns directly with the individual in question rather than use the 360 to avoid potentially painful confrontations.

## Build a culture of trust and candor.

According to many executives, successful use of the 360 rests on a foundation of trust and candor. For example, at Ford Europe, a 360 recipient can nominate his reviewers. To prevent a recipient from trying to "stack the deck" in her favor, her supervisor must review and approve all nominations. In addition, Ford requires a wide array of respondents for each recipient: one to two supervisors, three to six peers, and three to eight direct reports. Finally, reviewers can decide whether to remain anonymous to the recipient. Charpentier says that about "20% of reviewers choose to sign their reports." Many recipients and reviewers, he notes, even discuss the rating process with each other.

Jim McCarthy of Tark, a manufacturing company, has taken additional steps to build trust and candor in his organization. His emphasis on openness stems from his firsthand experience with "being 360'd." "I suspect that people weren't totally honest," he says. "There was a lot of praise—and I'm no saint." McCarthy has dramatically changed the way he communicates with managers and employees. Whereas he previously avoided painful conversations and protected people from troubling news about the company's overall performance, he now makes honest announcements about the business. "If they don't hear what I hear, they can't respond by making continuous improvements in their performance," he says. So far, he has received encouraging responses. "People have responded like adults," he says. "They've been very accepting."

**Reprint U0401A**

# About the Contributors

**Monci J. Williams** is a contributor to *Harvard Management Update*.

**Peter L. Allen** is a New York City–based writer, editor, and management consultant whose books have been published by the University of Pennsylvania Press and the University of Chicago Press.

**Karen Carney** is a contributor to *Harvard Management Update*.

**Michael E. Hattersley** is a contributor to *Harvard Management Update*.

**Loren Gary** is a contributor to *Harvard Management Update*.

**Lauren Keller Johnson** is a contributor to *Harvard Management Update*.

**Jennifer McFarland** is a contributor to *Harvard Management Update*.

**Hal Plotkin** is a writer and editor based in Palo Alto, California. The former editor of *Entrepreneur of the Year* magazine, he currently writes a regular column for the *San Francisco Chronicle*'s SFgate.com.

**Constantine von Hoffman** is a contributor to *Harvard Management Update*.

**Edward Prewitt** is a contributor to *Harvard Management Update*.

# Harvard Business Review Paperback Series

The Harvard Business Review Paperback Series offers the best thinking on cutting-edge management ideas from the world's leading thinkers, researchers, and managers. Designed for leaders who believe in the power of ideas to change business, these books will be useful to managers at all levels of experience, but especially senior executives and general managers. In addition, this series is widely used in training and executive development programs.

These books are priced at US$19.95
Price subject to change.

| Title | Product # |
| --- | --- |
| Harvard Business Review **Interviews with CEOs** | 3294 |
| Harvard Business Review on **Advances in Strategy** | 8032 |
| Harvard Business Review on **Appraising Employee Performance** | 7685 |
| Harvard Business Review on **Becoming a High Performance Manager** | 1296 |
| Harvard Business Review on **Brand Management** | 1445 |
| Harvard Business Review on **Breakthrough Leadership** | 8059 |
| Harvard Business Review on **Breakthrough Thinking** | 181X |
| Harvard Business Review on **Building Personal and Organizational Resilience** | 2721 |
| Harvard Business Review on **Business and the Environment** | 2336 |
| Harvard Business Review on **The Business Value of IT** | 9121 |
| Harvard Business Review on **Change** | 8842 |
| Harvard Business Review on **Compensation** | 701X |
| Harvard Business Review on **Corporate Ethics** | 273X |
| Harvard Business Review on **Corporate Governance** | 2379 |
| Harvard Business Review on **Corporate Responsibility** | 2748 |
| Harvard Business Review on **Corporate Strategy** | 1429 |
| Harvard Business Review on **Crisis Management** | 2352 |
| Harvard Business Review on **Culture and Change** | 8369 |
| Harvard Business Review on **Customer Relationship Management** | 6994 |
| Harvard Business Review on **Decision Making** | 5572 |

To order, call 1-800-668-6780, or go online at www.HBSPress.org

| Title | Product # |
|---|---|
| Harvard Business Review on **Developing Leaders** | 5003 |
| Harvard Business Review on **Doing Business in China** | 6387 |
| Harvard Business Review on **Effective Communication** | 1437 |
| Harvard Business Review on **Entrepreneurship** | 9105 |
| Harvard Business Review on **Finding and Keeping the Best People** | 5564 |
| Harvard Business Review on **Innovation** | 6145 |
| Harvard Business Review on **The Innovative Enterprise** | 130X |
| Harvard Business Review on **Knowledge Management** | 8818 |
| Harvard Business Review on **Leadership** | 8834 |
| Harvard Business Review on **Leadership at the Top** | 2756 |
| Harvard Business Review on **Leadership in a Changed World** | 5011 |
| Harvard Business Review on **Leading in Turbulent Times** | 1806 |
| Harvard Business Review on **Managing Diversity** | 7001 |
| Harvard Business Review on **Managing High-Tech Industries** | 1828 |
| Harvard Business Review on **Managing People** | 9075 |
| Harvard Business Review on **Managing Projects** | 6395 |
| Harvard Business Review on **Managing the Value Chain** | 2344 |
| Harvard Business Review on **Managing Uncertainty** | 9083 |
| Harvard Business Review on **Managing Your Career** | 1318 |
| Harvard Business Review on **Marketing** | 8040 |
| Harvard Business Review on **Measuring Corporate Performance** | 8826 |
| Harvard Business Review on **Mergers and Acquisitions** | 5556 |
| Harvard Business Review on **Mind of the Leader** | 6409 |
| Harvard Business Review on **Motivating People** | 1326 |
| Harvard Business Review on **Negotiation** | 2360 |
| Harvard Business Review on **Nonprofits** | 9091 |
| Harvard Business Review on **Organizational Learning** | 6153 |
| Harvard Business Review on **Strategic Alliances** | 1334 |
| Harvard Business Review on **Strategies for Growth** | 8850 |
| Harvard Business Review on **Teams That Succeed** | 502X |
| Harvard Business Review on **Turnarounds** | 6366 |
| Harvard Business Review on **What Makes a Leader** | 6374 |
| Harvard Business Review on **Work and Life Balance** | 3286 |

To order, call 1-800-668-6780, or go online at www.HBSPress.org

# Harvard Business Essentials

In the fast-paced world of business today, everyone needs a personal resource—a place to go for advice, coaching, background information, or answers. The Harvard Business Essentials series fits the bill. Concise and straightforward, these books provide highly practical advice for readers at all levels of experience. Whether you are a new manager interested in expanding your skills or an experienced executive looking to stay on top, these solution-oriented books give you the reliable tips and tools you need to improve your performance and get the job done. Harvard Business Essentials titles will quickly become your constant companions and trusted guides.

**These books are priced at US$19.95, except as noted.**
**Price subject to change.**

| Title | Product # |
|---|---|
| Harvard Business Essentials: **Negotiation** | 1113 |
| Harvard Business Essentials: **Managing Creativity and Innovation** | 1121 |
| Harvard Business Essentials: **Managing Change and Transition** | 8741 |
| Harvard Business Essentials: **Hiring and Keeping the Best People** | 875X |
| Harvard Business Essentials: **Finance for Managers** | 8768 |
| Harvard Business Essentials: **Business Communication** | 113X |
| Harvard Business Essentials: **Manager's Toolkit ($24.95)** | 2896 |
| Harvard Business Essentials: **Managing Projects Large and Small** | 3213 |
| Harvard Business Essentials: **Creating Teams with an Edge** | 290X |
| Harvard Business Essentials: **Entrepreneur's Toolkit** | 4368 |
| Harvard Business Essentials: **Coaching and Mentoring** | 435X |
| Harvard Business Essentials: **Crisis Management** | 4376 |
| Harvard Business Essentials: **Time Management** | 6336 |
| Harvard Business Essentials: **Power, Influence, and Persuasion** | 631X |
| Harvard Business Essentials: **Strategy** | 6328 |
| Harvard Business Essentials: **Decision Making** | 7618 |
| Harvard Business Essentials: **Marketer's Toolkit** | 7626 |
| Harvard Business Essentials: **Performance Management** | 9428 |

# The Results-Driven Manager

The Results-Driven Manager series collects timely articles from *Harvard Management Update* and *Harvard Management Communication Letter* to help senior to middle managers sharpen their skills, increase their effectiveness, and gain a competitive edge. Presented in a concise, accessible format to save managers valuable time, these books offer authoritative insights and techniques for improving job performance and achieving immediate results.

**These books are priced at US$14.95**
**Price subject to change.**

| Title | Product # |
|---|---|
| The Results-Driven Manager:<br>**Face-to-Face Communications for Clarity and Impact** | 3477 |
| The Results-Driven Manager:<br>**Managing Yourself for the Career You Want** | 3469 |
| The Results-Driven Manager:<br>**Presentations That Persuade and Motivate** | 3493 |
| The Results-Driven Manager: **Teams That Click** | 3507 |
| The Results-Driven Manager:<br>**Winning Negotiations That Preserve Relationships** | 3485 |
| The Results-Driven Manager: **Dealing with Difficult People** | 6344 |
| The Results-Driven Manager: **Taking Control of Your Time** | 6352 |
| The Results-Driven Manager: **Getting People on Board** | 6360 |
| The Results-Driven Manager:<br>**Motivating People for Improved Performance** | 7790 |
| The Results-Driven Manager: **Becoming an Effective Leader** | 7804 |
| The Results-Driven Manager:<br>**Managing Change to Reduce Resistance** | 7812 |
| The Results-Driven Manager:<br>**Hiring Smart for Competitive Advantage** | 9726 |
| The Results-Driven Manager:<br>**Retaining Your Best People** | 9734 |
| The Results-Driven Manager:<br>**Business Etiquette for the New Workplace** | 9742 |

To order, call 1-800-668-6780, or go online at www.HBSPress.org

# Management Dilemmas: Case Studies from the Pages of Harvard Business Review

When facing a difficult management challenge, wouldn't it be great if you could turn to a panel of experts to help guide you to the right decision? Now you can, with books from the Management Dilemmas series. Drawn from the pages of Harvard Business Review, each insightful guide poses a range of familiar and perplexing business situations and shares the wisdom of a small group of leading experts on how each of them would resolve the problem. Engagingly written, these interactive, solutions-oriented collections allow readers to match wits with the experts. They are designed to help managers hone their instincts and problem-solving skills to make sound judgment calls on everyday management dilemmas.

**These books are priced at US$19.95**
**Price subject to change.**

| Title | Product # |
|---|---|
| Management Dilemmas: **When Change Comes Undone** | 5038 |
| Management Dilemmas: **When Good People Behave Badly** | 5046 |
| Management Dilemmas: **When Marketing Becomes a Minefield** | 290X |
| Management Dilemmas: **When People Are the Problem** | 7138 |
| Management Dilemmas: **When Your Strategy Stalls** | 712X |

## How to Order

Harvard Business School Press publications are available worldwide
from your local bookseller or online retailer.
You can also call

### 1-800-668-6780

Our product consultants are available to help you
8:00 a.m.–6:00 p.m., Monday–Friday, Eastern Time.
Outside the U.S. and Canada, call: 617-783-7450
Please call about special discounts for quantities greater than ten.

You can order online at

### www.HBSPress.org